ジェフさんの歌で学ぶ
今日から使える英語表現
400

Inside The World Of A Boy And A Girl

ジェフリー・ウデン　登内和夫　著
Music BY : Geoffrey Wooden

SOGO HOREI Publishing Co., Ltd

はじめに

　歌で英語を学ぶ——大変楽しく有効な学習方法として、今までに試されたことがある方も多いことと思います。私自身、英語を学び始める前から、ビートルズ、カーペンターズ、サイモン＆ガーファンクル等の曲を、意味も分からないままひたすら聴き続け、そのお陰で、英語らしいリズムや発音を自然に身に付けることができました。

　確かに、英語らしい発音を自然に身に付けるという意味では、既存のポップスを聴くということは大いに役に立つものであると思います。しかし、英語の表現力や文法力を身に付けるという観点から見るとどうでしょうか？　必ずしも効率的な方法であるとは言えないのではないでしょうか？

　その理由は大きく分けて3つあります。

　1……既存のポップスは日本人が英語を学ぶために作られたものではない。そのため、歌詞の中に日本人が学ぶべき表現があまり入っていなかったり、スラングが多過ぎたり、言葉遊びが多くて、歌詞自体にあまり意味のないものがあったりといったことがあり、歌で英語を勉強しようとしても、あまり実用的な英語力が得られない。
　2……歌詞は一種の芸術作品であるため、言葉に様々な意味合いが込められていることが多い。そのため、訳者にいくら力があっても、作者に真意を確かめない限り、歌詞の本当の意味が分からない場合も多く、訳を見ても何を言っているか分からないことがよくある。
　3……歌詞に出てくる表現は、あくまでもその歌詞の文脈の中で用いられているのであり、それが実際の会話の中でどう使われるのかという実用的な側面が分かりづらい。

　以上のような問題点を克服し、歌を使って英語を学習するための理想的な形を提供するのが本書です。その特徴を次に挙げてみます。

　1……1つのテーマに基づいて、全曲が本書のためにオリジナル制作されたものである。
　2……1曲毎にサブテーマが定められており、曲調もそれに応じたものとな

っている。そして、サブテーマに沿った英語表現が、曲の至る所に散りばめられており、曲調に合わせて様々な表現が覚えられるようになっている。

3……歌詞の分かりづらい部分を正確に読み解くための解説がなされている。

4……歌詞に出てくる表現が、日常会話でどう用いられるかを示すために、そうした表現を用いた対話を載せることで、実用的な英語力がつくようになっている。

さあ、本書を使って、英語の歌を聴き、一緒に歌うことで、自然に実用的な英語表現を身に付ける楽しさを味わってください。

本書が完成するまでには、多くの方々のお力をお借りしました。本書の企画段階から完成に至るまで、惜しみない援助をしてくださった総合法令出版の竹下祐治さんと斉藤由希さん、原稿執筆段階で様々なアドバイスをくださった渡邊紘子さんと Emi Wooden さん、Sax で曲作りに参加してくれた Tim Green さん、そして、本書を通じて楽しみながら英語を習得しようとしてくださっている読者の皆様に、心より感謝申し上げます。

2008 年 9 月 25 日
登内　和夫

学習にあたって

♪ *Inside The World Of A Boy And A Girl* について

　本書の付属 CD には、本書のために作られたオリジナル曲が 8 曲収録されていますが、そのアルバムタイトルが *Inside The World Of A Boy And A Girl* です。

　Inside The World Of A Boy And A Girl は、8 曲で一つのストーリーをなすテーマアルバムですが、そのストーリーは次のようなものです。

　ある男性が、ある女性に恋をする。そして、あれこれ思い悩みながらもその恋が成就し、幸せな時を迎えるが、やがて些細な心のすれ違いから、互いを激しく非難し合う中で別れの危機を迎える。彼女を失いそうになる深い悲しみの中で、男性が素直に自分のしたことを謝罪することにより、二人の関係は修復に向かう。こうした一連の流れを経験することで、その男性は人生や愛というものについて、より深い洞察を身に付けていく。

　1 曲 1 曲がストーリーの一部を担う形で、それにふさわしい曲調と歌詞を持っています。読者の皆さんは、各曲の持つ雰囲気を感じ取りながら、歌を聴き、一緒に歌う中で、自然に実用的な英語表現を身に付けていくことになります。

　Inside The World Of A Boy And A Girl は、全曲が Geoffrey Wooden によって作詞・作曲され、Geoffrey の自宅スタジオで制作・録音されました。なお、8 曲目のサックスソロのみ、Tim Green によるものです。

　Geoffrey Wooden はオレゴン大学で作曲法を学んだ後、ブリティッシュコロンビア大学で作曲法の修士号を取得しました。在学中は、BMI Student Composer's Award において、700 名以上の参加者の中で第 3 位に輝いたこともある音楽の才人です。

　そんな Geoffrey Wooden の作った *Inside The World Of A Boy And A Girl* は、キャッチーなメロディーがぎっしり詰まった、聴けば聴くほど味わいが出てくる素敵なアルバムです。そして、男性読者にとっては、ご自分の恋愛体験と共通するものを見つけて、思わずニヤリとしてしまうこともあるでしょう。また、女性読者にとっては、恋愛における男性心理を勉強するいい素材となるに違いありません。是非、繰り返し聴いて、恋も英語も楽しく勉強していただければと思います。

本書の構成

　「ジェフさんの歌で学ぶ　今日から使える英語表現４００」は、歌詞、対訳、曲解説、学習用歌詞、語句解説、重要表現の６つのパートから成り立っています。ここでは、それぞれのパートの特徴、注意点等を説明していきます。

♪歌詞…………歌詞は、基本的にはメロディーの切れ目に合わせて改行されており、必ずしも１行に１つの文になっているわけではありません。通常のCDの歌詞カードなどでは、コンマやピリオドなども全て省かれる場合が多いので、どこからどこまでが１つの文であるかを把握することすら難しい場合が多々あります。そこで本書では、コンマとピリオドを入れ、どこからどこまでが１つの文であるかを明確に示すようにしてあります。

♪対訳…………通常の歌詞訳は、様々な制約がある中で、芸術性を追求しているため、元の英語の意味が分かりづらくなっている場合もよくあります。本書は学習書であるため、芸術性よりは、元の英語の意味がきちんと分かるということを第一に訳をつけてあります。

　しかし、意味がはっきりわかる場合は、多少の意訳をしてある場合もあります。そのような場合でも、他のパートで直訳が分かるようにしてあります。

　また、対訳ということで、英語の１行に対して１行の日本語訳をあててありますので、英語の語順に沿った理解ができるようになっています。

♪曲解説………その曲のアルバムの中での位置付けや曲調の説明、曲中に出てくる表現を使っての歌詞の要約が載っています。曲を理解する助けにしてください。

♪学習用歌詞……「歌詞」の所で説明したように、本書の歌詞にはコンマやピリオドが付いているので、通常の歌詞に比べて文の単位が分かりやすくなっています。それでも、実際の文では不要なコンマがあったり、各行の頭が全て大文字で書かれて

いたりしているので、一つひとつの文がすぐに分かるというわけにはいきません。そこで、歌詞用の表記ではなく、普通の英文の表記に直して、その点を分かりやすくしたものが学習用歌詞です。
そして、語句解説に出てくる表現には波線を施した上で、アルファベットを付け、重要表現に出てくる表現については、赤字にした上で、数字を付してあります。

♪語句解説………歌詞の中に出てくる分かりづらい表現や文法事項を説明しているパートです。このパートを読むことで歌詞の正確な理解が可能になるので、是非目を通してください。

♪重要表現………歌詞の中に出てくる重要表現を意味と共に示し、それらの会話での使用例を示す対話を載せてあるパートです。
対話の下には、その対話中に出てきた重要表現も抜き出してあります。
さらに、そうした表現の中で、スラングに近く、公式の場や目上の人に対して使うべきでない表現については、【卑】という印を付けておきました。使用の目安にしてください。
　なお、歌詞の中に出てくる重要表現については、歌詞の中に出てくる順に、対話に出てくる重要表現については、対話の中に出てくる順に載せてあります。

本書で使用されている記号は、次のような意味を表しています。
- S ……… 主語
- V ……… 動詞
- O ……… 目的語
- C ……… 補語
- － ……… 動詞の原形
- －ing … 動詞のing形（現在分詞または動名詞）
- p.p. …… 過去分詞
- ～ ……… 名詞、代名詞、形容詞、副詞等（ひとつの英語表現の中で、これらの語が２つ出てくる時には、２つ目のものを〈…〉という記号で表しています。）

CONTENTS

はじめに ……………………………………………… 1
学習にあたって ……………………………………… 3

▶ **SONG #1** / **Head Over Heels** — 9

歌詞と対訳 …………………………………………… 10
曲解説 ………………………………………………… 12
学習用歌詞 …………………………………………… 13
語句解説 ……………………………………………… 16
重要表現 ……………………………………………… 19

▶ **SONG #2** / **I Want…** — 29

歌詞と対訳 …………………………………………… 30
曲解説 ………………………………………………… 32
学習用歌詞 …………………………………………… 33
語句解説 ……………………………………………… 36
重要表現 ……………………………………………… 88

▶ **SONG #3** / **Fall Into Place** — 47

歌詞と対訳 …………………………………………… 48
曲解説 ………………………………………………… 50
学習用歌詞 …………………………………………… 51
語句解説 ……………………………………………… 53
重要表現 ……………………………………………… 56

▶ **SONG #4** / **Nothing You Can Do** — 65

歌詞と対訳 …………………………………………… 66
曲解説 ………………………………………………… 68
学習用歌詞 …………………………………………… 69
語句解説 ……………………………………………… 71
重要表現 ……………………………………………… 73

▶ SONG #5 / Go On! Get Out! — 81

歌詞と対訳 ……………………………………… 82
曲解説 …………………………………………… 84
学習用歌詞 ……………………………………… 85
語句解説 ………………………………………… 88
重要表現 ………………………………………… 89

▶ SONG #6 / I'm Sorry — 99

歌詞と対訳 ……………………………………… 100
曲解説 …………………………………………… 102
学習用歌詞 ……………………………………… 103
語句解説 ………………………………………… 106
重要表現 ………………………………………… 107

▶ SONG #7 / Take A Step Back — 113

歌詞と対訳 ……………………………………… 114
曲解説 …………………………………………… 116
学習用歌詞 ……………………………………… 117
語句解説 ………………………………………… 119
重要表現 ………………………………………… 121

▶ SONG #8 / Don't Give Up — 127

歌詞と対訳 ……………………………………… 128
曲解説 …………………………………………… 130
学習用歌詞 ……………………………………… 131
語句解説 ………………………………………… 134
重要表現 ………………………………………… 135

索引 ……………………………………………… 144

▶ **SONG #1**
Head Over Heels

▶ SONG #1

Head Over Heels

(Verse 1)
I've got butterflies in my stomach.
My heart just skipped a beat.
From the moment that I saw you,
I was swept off my feet.

Now my head's in the clouds,
And I've forgotten all about,
All the things I need to do.
The only thing I think about is you.

I'd love to take you out,
For a night on the town.
You and me together,
Just cruising around.

What do you wanna do?
Anything's fine with me.
I wanna hang out with you,
So let's kick back and shoot the breeze.

(Chorus)
I'm so crazy about you,
I don't know what to do.
I've fallen head over heels.
I've been swept off my feet.
I wanna tell you how I feel,
But I'm too shy to speak.
Every time I see you,
My knees get weak.
And now I've got to know, I've got to know,
I've got to know, I've got to know.
Are you crazy about me?
Are you crazy about me?

(Verse 2)
I'm in seventh heaven.
I'm floating on cloud nine.
If I could say the right words,
In no time you'd be mine.

But I don't know what to say.
I could ask you, "What's new?"
Or "Hi, how's it going?"
But neither of these will do.

I'd rather tell you something like,
"You mean the world to me."
But I'm afraid that if I say it,
I'll push you away from me.

I guess I should be patient.
I guess I should just wait.
I don't want to rush things,
But I don't wanna hesitate.

(Chorus)

(Bridge)
What would you do if you were in my shoes?
Would you take a chance, ask her to dance?
Or would you wait and see because maybe
someday, maybe someday,
Maybe someday she'll ask me?
Maybe someday she'll ask me?

(Verse 3)
One of these days I'll say it.
I'll spill my guts to you,
After I've gathered up my courage,
After thinking it through and through.

I don't know what you will think.
Don't know how you'll react.
But once it's out in the open,
It's too late to take it back.

So I'll just put it out there,
And wait for your reply.
Waiting may just kill me,
But I know it's worth a try.

I pray to god you'll tell me,
Something along the lines of,
"Why don't we have a drink?"
And I'll completely lose my mind.

(Chorus)

Are you crazy about me?

(Verse 1)
緊張してそわそわしてる僕
高鳴る胸
君を見た瞬間から
夢中になってしまった

今はもう全く集中できない
全てを忘れてしまっている
しなくちゃいけないはずのこと　すべてを
たったひとつ君のことを考えている

君を連れ出したいよ
夜の街に
僕と君は一緒
ただあちこちぶらつきたい

君はどうしたい？
僕は何でも構わない
ただ君と一緒にいたいんだ
だからのんびりお喋りでもしようよ

(Chorus)
君に夢中で
僕はどうしていいかわからない
すっかり恋に落ちてしまった
ずっと夢中なんだ
僕の気持ちを君に伝えたい
でも恥ずかしくて話せない
君を見るといつも
緊張で膝が震えちゃう
僕は知らなきゃならないんだ
どうしても知らなくちゃ
君は僕のことが好き？
僕のことが

(Verse 2)
僕は本当に幸せだよ
夢のような気分さ
もしうまく言えたなら
すぐに君は僕のもの

でも　なんて言ったらいいんだろう
僕が聞けることといったら　「最近どう？」
「やあ、元気？」くらい
でもこれじゃあダメなんだ

いっそ　こんなことを言ってしまいたい
「君は僕のすべてだ」
でも怖いのはもしそんなことを言ったら
君を追いやってしまうということ

たぶん僕は我慢するべきなんだろう
ただただ待つべきなんだろう
事を急ぎたくない
でもためらったりはしたくない

(Chorus)

(Bridge)
もし僕の立場だったらどうする？
いちかばちか　彼女をダンスに誘う？
それとも　待つ？　だって
いつか　いつの日か
いつか彼女が誘ってくれるかもしれないから
いつか彼女が誘ってくれるかもしれないから

(Verse 3)
いつかそのうち僕は言うよ
君に思いのたけをすべてぶつけてみる
勇気をかき集め
よくよく考えた後にね

君がなんて思うかわからない
君がどんな風に反応するかなんてわからない
でも一度言ってしまったら
もう取り消せはしない

だから僕の気持ちをすべて伝えて
あとは君の返事を待つ
待つのは辛いかもしれないけど
トライしてみる価値があることはわかってる

君が僕に言ってくれることを神に祈る
こんな感じのこと
「ちょっと飲みに行かない？」
そしたら僕は完全におかしくなるね

(Chorus)

君は僕のことが好き？

▶ SONG #1　Head Over Heels

曲解説

　ある男性が、ある女性に恋をする。そして、あれこれ思い悩みながらもその恋が成就し、幸せな時を迎えるが、やがて些細な心のすれ違いから、互いを激しく非難し合う中で別れの危機を迎える。彼女を失いそうになる深い悲しみの中で、男性が素直に自分のしたことを謝罪することにより、二人の関係は修復に向かう。こうした一連の流れを経験することで、その男性は人生や愛というものについて、より深い洞察を身に付けていく。

　1つの恋をめぐっての、ある男性の心の変化とその成長をテーマにしたアルバム **Inside The World Of A Boy And A Girl** の1曲目を飾る **Head Over Heels**。この曲では、アルバムの主人公が、ある女性に恋をした際の心の状態が表現されています。好きだけどどうしていいか分からない。恋の初期段階特有の、期待と不安が入り混じった心理状態が、この曲のテーマです。

　曲の冒頭、オルガンの音だけをバックに、主人公が高らかに恋の宣言をします (**I've got butterflies in my stomach. My heart just skipped a beat. From the moment that I saw you, I was swept off my feet.**)。

　主人公は恋のことで頭が一杯で、何にも集中することができません (**Now my head's in the clouds.**)。そして、恋する気持ちが強過ぎるあまり、どうしていいか分からなくなってしまいます (**I'm so crazy about you I don't know what to do.**)。気持ちを伝えようにも、恥ずかしくて話しかけられないし (**I wanna tell you how I feel, but I'm too shy to speak.**)、彼女を見るたびに、緊張で膝が震えてしまう有様です (**Every time I see you, my knees get weak.**)。

　恋の成就に可能性を見出したかと思うと (**If I could say the right words, in no time you'd be mine.**)、告白することで彼女を遠ざけてしまうことを恐れたりもします (**I'd rather tell you something like, "You mean the world to me." But I'm afraid that if I say it, I'll push you away from me.**)。

　しかし、ついに主人公は彼女に告白することを決意します (**So I'll just put it out there.**)。色よい返事を期待して (**I pray to god you'll tell me something along the lines of, "Why don't we have a drink?"**)。

I. 学習用歌詞

(Verse 1)
I've got butterflies in my stomach.
  1

My heart just **skipped a beat**.
2

From the moment that I saw you, **I was swept off my feet**.
A   3

Now **my head's in the clouds**, and I've forgotten all about all the things
     4   B
I need to do.
The only thing I think about is you.

I'd love to **take** you **out for** a **night on the town**.
       C   5   5

You and me together, just **cruising around**.
D   E6

What do you wanna do?
            F

Anything's fine with me.
7
I wanna **hang out** with you, so let's **kick back** and **shoot the breeze**.
     7   8   5

(Chorus)
I'm so **crazy about** you I don't know what to do.
  G9   H

I've **fallen head over heels**.
   9

I've been swept off my feet.
I wanna tell you how I feel, but I'm **too** shy **to** speak.
                               10

Every time I see you, **my knees get weak**.
9   9
And now I've got to know, I've got to know, I've got to know, I've got to know.
       I

Are you crazy about me?
Are you crazy about me?

SONG #1 Head Over Heels

(Verse 2)
I'**m in seventh heaven**.
 11
I'm **floating on cloud nine**.
     11

If I could say the right words, **in no time** you'd be mine.
 J   12

But I don't know what to say.
I could ask you, "**What's new**?" or "Hi, **how's it going**?" but neither of these **will**
 K   13   13   L   14
 do.

I'**d rather** tell you something like, "You mean the world to me."
 15
But I'm afraid that if I say it, I'll **push** you **away from** me.
                                         16

I guess I should be patient.
 4
I guess I should just wait.
I don't want to **rush things**, but I don't wanna hesitate.
                  17
(Chorus)

(Bridge)
What would you do if you **were in my shoes**?
                           18
Would you **take a chance**, ask her to dance?
           19
Or would you **wait and see** because maybe someday, maybe someday,
             20
maybe someday she'll ask me, maybe someday she'll ask me?
                  M

(Verse 3)
One of these days I'll say it.
 21   N
I'll **spill my guts** to you after I've **gathered up my courage**, after **thinking** it
     22   22   23
through and through.

I don't know what you will think.
　　　　　 ‾‾‾‾‾‾‾‾‾‾‾‾‾‾‾‾
　　　　　　　O

Don't know how you'll react.
But **once** it**'s out in the open**, it's too late to **take it back**.
　　　24　　　25　　　　　　　　　　　　　　26

So I'll just **put it out there**, and wait for your reply.
　　　　　　　18
Waiting may just **kill** me, but I know it's **worth a try**.
‾‾‾‾‾‾‾　　　　　27　　　　　　　　　28
P

I pray to god you'll tell me **something along the lines of**, "**Why don't we** have a
　　　　　　　　　　　　　　　　　29　　　　　　　　　　　　　30
drink?" and I'll completely lose my mind.

(Chorus)

Are you crazy about me?

▶SONG #1　Head Over Heels

II. 語句解説

A. From the moment that I saw you
　この that は関係副詞で、when と同様の働きをしており、that 以下が直前の moment を修飾しています。「瞬間」とはどういう瞬間かというと、「僕が君を見た」瞬間ということです。

　この部分は、from the moment と and then I saw you という2つが、and then が関係副詞 that に置き換わることによって1つにつながったものと考えることができます。逆に言えば、関係副詞を含む形が出てきた場合、関係副詞を〈接続詞＋副詞〉に置き換えれば、前から後ろに意味を取っていくことができます。From the moment that I saw you について言えば、まず moment までを「瞬間から」と解釈し、that を and＋then に置き換えて、「それで、その時に僕は君を見たんだけど」と考えるわけです。

B. all the things I need to do
　things の後ろに目的格の関係代名詞 that が省略されており、その that 以下が直前の things を修飾しています。「物事」とはどういう物事かというと、「僕がする必要のある」物事ということです。

　省略されている that の後ろを見ると、I need to do となっており、do の後ろにあるべき目的語がありません。その目的語（実際には the things）が接続詞の働きも兼ねて関係代名詞 that に姿を変えて I の前に出たのです。

　関係代名詞を含む文が出てきた場合、ここで説明したように、関係代名詞以下が直前の名詞（先行詞といいます）を修飾する形で処理してもいいのですが、関係代名詞を〈接続詞＋代名詞〉に置き換えて、前から後ろに意味を取る形で処理することもできます。all the things I need to do について言えば、まず things までを「全ての物事」と解釈し、省略されている that を and＋them に置き換えて、「それで、それらを僕はやる必要があるんだけど」と考えるわけです。

C. would love to
　would love to は would like to と同様「―したい」という意味ですが、would love to は、したい気持ちがより強い場合に用いられます。would love to は女性が用いる表現だという説明も見られますが、男性も用います。

D. You and me together
　この部分の前には、I'd like it to be とか It would be といった語句が省略されています。

このitはその場の状況を漠然と表すitです。

E. cruising
　このing形は現在分詞で、分詞構文を作っています。分詞構文は主節内の動詞を修飾する副詞句として働いて、「－する時」、「－するので」、「－するけれど」、「－しながら」等様々な意味を表わします。また、単にand－ということで後ろにつながっていく用法もあり、ここもその用法です。つまり、「君と僕は一緒、そしてただぶらついて回る」ということです。

F. wanna
　wannaはwant toをその発音に基づいて略して綴ったものです。going toがgonnaに、got toがgottaになるのも同様です。

G. I'm so crazy about you I don't know
　youとIの間にthatが省略されており、〈so ～ that SV〉で、「とても～なのでSはVする」という構文を作っています。この構文の場合、口語ではthatが省略されることがよくあります。

H. what to do
　〈疑問詞＋to－〉という形は、まず疑問詞を訳し、動詞を訳して最後に「べきか」をつける形で処理することができます。what to doなら、「何をするべきか」といった具合です。where to go、when to start、which to take等便利に使える表現です。

I. have got to
　have gotはhaveと同じなので、have got toはhave to（－しなければならない）ということです。

J. If I could say the right words, in no time you'd be mine.
　〈If S1 過去形, S2 would －.〉という形は、仮定法過去と呼ばれるもので、現在の事実に反する仮定や願望を言う形で、「(S1は実際には…しないのだが) もしS1が…したとしたら、S2は－するだろうに」という意味になります。ですから、この文の場合は、「(実際は、僕は上手い言葉を言えないんだけれど) もし僕が上手い言葉を言えたとしたら、すぐに君は僕のものになるのに」ということです。

▶ SONG #1　Head Over Heels

K. could
　このcouldもJで説明した仮定法過去の用法として用いられています。すなわち、「もし自分がその気になれば、−できるんだけれど」とか、「もしチャンスがあれば、−できるんだけれど」ということです。ここでは、「もし自分がその気になれば（もしチャンスがあれば）」という部分は実際には言葉に表わされていません。このように仮定法においては、if節を表に出さなかったり、if節以外の形で仮定条件を表現することがよく見られます。

L. neither of
　neither of 〜 は、「〜のどちらも−ない」という意味で全部否定になっています。

M. she'll ask me
　このBridgeの部分は、この曲の主人公が、自分以外の一般の人達youに、もし自分と同じ立場にいたらどうするかを尋ねている部分であり、ここでのmeは文脈からいえばyouになるはずです。しかし、この主人公であるIが、この部分で再度自分のこととして問題を捉えなおしているので、youではなくmeを使っています。

N. it
　このitは、主人公の彼女に対する想いを指しています。

O. what you will think
　what you will think というのは、本来は what will you think? という疑問文ですが、I don't know の目的語として文の一部に組み入れられているため、whatの後ろが〈主語＋動詞〉の語順になっています。このようなものを間接疑問文と呼びます。

P. Waiting
　このing形は動名詞と呼ばれるもので、動詞を名詞化して「−すること」という意味になります。ここではWaitingが「待つこと」となって、文の主語になっています。

Ⅲ. 重要表現

① have got butterflies in one's stomach：(緊張して) ドキドキする、そわそわする

▶活用例

W : You look a little freaked out. What's up?
M : Oh, it's nothing too crazy. I've just got to give a speech at the wedding tonight.
W : Don't worry about it.
M : Yeah, I'm alright. I've just got butterflies in my stomach.

W：ちょっとパニくっているみたいね。どうしたの？
M：あー、別にたいしたことじゃないよ。ただ、今夜の結婚式でスピーチをしなくちゃならないんだ。
W：心配しなくても大丈夫よ。
M：うん、大丈夫。ただ、ちょっとドキドキしちゃって。

*freaked out：パニック状態に陥っている
*What's up?：どうしたの？　最近調子はどう？

② One's heart skips a beat.：心臓がドキッとする

▶活用例

W : Oh my god!
M : What?!
W : My dog almost got hit by that car!
M : No way! Is he OK?
W : Yeah, it looks like it, but my heart just skipped a beat.

W：わー！
M：どうした？！
W：私の犬が、もう少しであの車に轢かれるところだったの！
M：うそだろ！　大丈夫？
W：うん、大丈夫みたい。でもほんとに心臓がドキっとしたわ。

*Oh my god!：何てことだ！　信じられない！　まあ！
*get hit by ～：～に轢かれる
*No way!：まさか！

③ be swept off one's feet：(誰かに) 夢中になる

▶活用例

W : You seem upbeat.
M : Yeah, well, I met the most beautiful girl last night.
W : No way! Really? That's great!
M : Yeah, I was totally swept off my feet.

W：なんだか嬉しそうね。
M：うん、いやぁー、昨日の晩、最高にかわいい子に会ったんだよ。

SONG #1　Head Over Heels

W：うそー！　ほんとに？　すごいじゃない！
M：うん、もうほんとに夢中になっちゃった。

④ One's head is in the clouds.：夢想にふけって集中できない
I guess S V.：S は V すると思う

▶活用例
W : I'm a mess today.
M : Yeah, you do seem kind of out of it.
W : Well, I have a lot on my mind. I guess my head's just in the clouds.

W：今日は頭がグチャグチャ。
M：うん、なんだかボーっとしているみたいだね。
W：うーん、いろんなことが気になって。あれこれ空想ばかりして集中できない感じなの。

*kind of：ちょっと、なんだか
*out of it：ぼーっとして
*have ～ on one's mind：～を気にかけている

⑤ take ～ out for …：～を･･･に連れ出す
night on the town：夜の街で楽しむこと
shoot the breeze：おしゃべりする

▶活用例
W : So, what did you do on your date?
M : Well, I took her out for a night on the town.
W : Yeah, AND?
M : And that's it. We just had a couple of drinks and shot the breeze.

W：ところで、デートでは何したの？
M：うーんと、彼女を夜の街に連れ出したんだ。
W：うんうん、それで？
M：で、それだけ。軽く飲んで、おしゃべりしただけだよ。

⑥ cruise around：あちこち回る

▶活用例
W : Hey Jeff. Where are you?
M : I'm in Shinjuku.
W : What are you doing?
M : Nothing much. Just cruising around.

W：ねえ、ジェフ、今どこ？
M：新宿だよ。
W：何してんの？
M：別にたいしたことしてないよ。ただブラついてるだけ。

⑦ **Anything is fine with 〜．**：〜にとっては何でも構わない
hang out：時を過ごす、一緒にいる、ブラブラする

▶活用例
W：Are you busy on Saturday?
M：Not at all. You wanna hang out?
W：Yeah. What do you wanna do?
M：Oh, anything's fine with me.

W：土曜日は忙しい？
M：全然。一緒に過ごす？
W：うん。何したい？
M：うーん、僕は何でもいいけど。

⑧ **kick back**：のんびりする

▶活用例
W：Do you want to go dancing tonight?
M：Actually, I'm kind of tired.
W：Oh, OK. Then, what do you wanna do?
M：Do you mind if we just kick back and watch TV?
W：No, that's fine with me.

W：今夜踊りに行かない？
M：ほんとのこと言って、ちょっと疲れているんだ
W：そう、わかった。じゃあ、何がしたいの？
M：ただのんびりとテレビでも見るっていうのでもいいかなあ？
W：うん、私はいいわよ。

＊**Do you mind if S V?**　：**S** が **V** してもいいですか？

⑨ **be crazy about 〜**：〜に夢中になっている
fall head over heels：完全に恋に落ちる
every time S V：**S** が **V** するたびに
One's knees get weak.：（緊張して）膝がガクガクする

▶活用例
W：Sounds like you've really fallen for her.
M：Yep. Fallen head over heels.
W：Have you told her that yet?
M：That I'm crazy about her? No way. I'm too shy. My knees get weak every time I see her.

W：彼女に恋しちゃったって感じね。
M：うん。完全に参っちゃった。
W：彼女にはもう告白したの？
M：彼女に夢中だってこと？　まさかぁ。恥ずかし過ぎるよ。彼女に会うたび

SONG #1　Head Over Heels

に膝がガクガクしちゃうんだ。

*Sounds like S V.:〈話を聞いていると〉SはVするようだ
*fall for ～:～に恋する

⑩ too ～ to −:～過ぎて−できない

▶活用例
M : You seem kind of stressed out. Everything OK?
W : Yeah, but I have so much work to do!
M : Wanna take a coffee break?
W : I can't! I'm too busy to take a break!

M：ちょっとイライラしているみたいだけど。大丈夫？
W：うん、でもやらなきゃならない仕事がすごく沢山あって！
M：一休みする？
W：できないわ！　忙しすぎて、休憩なんかしてられないの！

⑪ be in seventh heaven:本当に幸せである
　 float on cloud nine:夢見心地である

▶活用例
W : Wow! What a beautiful day!!
M : Yeah, it feels so good to be outside.
W : Man, everything's perfect. I'm in seventh heaven.
M : And I'm floating on cloud nine.

W：わぁー！　なんていい天気なんでしょう！！
M：うん、外にいるのが本当に気持ちいいね。
W：うわぁ、全てが完璧ね。最高の気分よ。
M：僕も夢見心地だよ。

*It feels ～ to −.:−するのは～に感じられる

⑫ in no time:すぐに

▶活用例
M : Hello?
W : Hey, where are you?
M : I'm on my way. Sorry I'm late, but I'll be there in no time.

M：もしもし？
W：ねぇ、今どこ？
M：今向かっているところ。遅れてごめん、でもすぐ着くから。

*be on one's way:向かっているところだ

⑬ **What's new?**：最近、何かあった？
   How's it going?：最近どう？

▶活用例
M : Hey Amy. What's new?
W : Nothing much. How's it going with you?
M : Not bad. Pretty busy, though.

M：やぁ、エイミー。最近何かあった？
W：別に。あなたはどう？
M：まあまあだね。結構忙しいけど。

***not bad**：まあまあ良い

⑭ **～ will do.**：～で大丈夫

▶活用例
W : Do you have a pen I could borrow?
M : Just a sec. Um, I've just got this pencil.
W : Oh, that'll do. Thanks.

W：ペン貸してもらえる？
M：ちょっと待って。うーん、この鉛筆しか持ってないや。
W：うん、それで大丈夫。ありがとう。

***Just a sec.**：ちょっと待って

⑮ **would rather －**：むしろーしたい、ーするほうがいい

▶活用例
M : Do you feel like watching a movie tonight?
W : Actually, I'd rather go out for a drink.
M : Oh yeah? That sounds good to me!
W : Great! Let's go!

M：今夜は映画でも観る？
W：実際のところ、飲みに行くほうがいいなあ。
M：そうなの？　いいねー！
W：やった！　行きましょう！

***Feel like － ing?**：ーする？　ーしたい気分？
***go out for a drink**：飲みに行く

▶ SONG #1　Head Over Heels

⑯ push 〜 away from …：〜を・・・から追いやる

▶活用例
W : Amy seems a little upset. You guys OK?
M : Yeah, but I told her I need more time to myself.
W : Ah. I can imagine she wouldn't like that.
M : Yeah, it's tricky. I need some private time, but I don't want to push her away from me.

W：エイミーはちょっと怒っているみたいだけど。あなた達、大丈夫？
M：うん、でももっと自分の時間が欲しいって彼女に言っちゃったんだ。
W：あー。彼女は気に入らないでしょうね。
M：うん、ちょっと難しいんだけど。自分の時間が必要ではあるんだけど、彼女を遠ざけたくもないんだよね。

⑰ rush things：慌てて物事を行う

▶活用例
W : How was your date?
M : Good, until the end.
W : Why? What happened?
M : I tried to kiss her but she slapped me and said she didn't wanna rush things.

W：デートはどうだった？
M：良かったよ、最後以外はね。
W：なんで？　何があったの？
M：彼女にキスをしようとしたら、彼女が僕をひっぱたいて、そんなに事を急ぎたくないって言ったんだ。

⑱ be in one's shoes：〜と同じ立場に身を置く
　 put it out there：隠さずに全て話す

▶活用例
M : I'm not sure what to tell her.
W : Why don't you just put it out there and see what she says?
M : Is that what you would do?
W : Yeah, if I were in your shoes.

M：彼女に何て言ったらいいか、よくわからなくて。
W：とりあえず気持ちを全部伝えて、彼女が何て言うか確かめてみたら？
M：君だったらそうするかい？
W：うん、もし私があなたの立場だったらね。

*Why don't you − ? ：−したらどうですか？
*what S V：S が V すること

24

⑲ **take a chance**：いちかばちかやってみる

▶活用例
M : Did you audition for that part on the TV show yet?
W : No, I don't think I'm going to even try.
M : Why not?
W : Oh, I'm sure they won't choose me.
M : Well, you never know. You should give it a try. Come on. Take a chance.

M：例のテレビ番組のあの役のオーディションはもう受けた？
W：ううん。行くのもやめようかなあって思ってるの。
M：どうして？
W：うん、きっと私は選ばれないから。
M：うーん、やってみなきゃわからないじゃない。受けてみたほうがいいよ。さあ、いちかばちか、やってみなよ。

***audition for 〜**：〜のオーディションを受ける
***Why not?**：どうして（しないの）？
***You never know.**：先のことはわからないよ
***Come on.**：さあさあ

⑳ **wait and see**：成り行きを見守る

▶活用例
M : Do you think Tim will be able to get enough tickets for the concert?
W : I don't know. I heard they're all sold out already.
M : Well, he's pretty good at finding things online.
W : Yeah, that's true. I guess we'll just have to wait and see.

M：ティムは、そのコンサートのチケットを人数分取れると思う？
W：わからないわ。もう売り切れたとも聞いているし。
M：でも彼、ネットで色々見つけるのが結構得意じゃない。
W：ええ、確かに。今はただ様子を見守るしかないわね。

***be sold out**：売り切れだ
***be good at － ing**：—するのが得意だ

㉑ **one of these days**：いつかそのうち

▶活用例
M : I'm gonna quit smoking next week.
W : Uh-huh, I've heard that before.
M : I know, but one of these days I'll really do it.
W : Well, I'm not holding my breath.

SONG #1　Head Over Heels

M：来週には禁煙するよ。
W：はいはい、前にもそれ聞いたわよ。
M：そうだね。でも、そのうちいつか、本当にやめるよ。
W：まぁ、期待してないけどね。

*be gonna －：ーするだろう、ーするつもりだ
*quit － ing：ーするのをやめる
*hold one's breath：期待して待つ

㉒ spill one's guts：全て話す
　gather up one's courage：勇気を奮い起こす

▶活用例
W : Have you said anything to her yet?
M : Yeah, I told her everything.
W : Everything?!
M : Yep. I gathered up my courage and completely spilled my guts.

W：彼女にもう何か言った？
M：うん、全部話したよ。
W：全部？！
M：うん。勇気を振り絞って、自分の思っていることを全部伝えたんだ。

㉓ think it through：とことん考える

▶活用例
W : Have you decided which pair of shoes you're going to buy?
M : No, not yet. I need more time to think it through.
W : Are you serious? You've been looking at shoes for two hours!
M : Yeah, I know. Sorry, but I'm picky.

W：どっちの靴を買うか決めた？
M：いや、まだ決めてない。よく考える時間がもう少し必要なんだ。
W：本気？　もう2時間も見ているのよ。
M：うん、わかってる。ごめんね、でも僕は好みがうるさいんだ。

*picky：好みがうるさい

㉔ once S V：ひとたび S が V すると

▶活用例
W : Have you cleaned the bathroom yet?
M : No, not yet.
W : Well, when are you gonna do it?
M : I'll do it once I finish washing the dishes.

W：浴室はもう掃除した？
M：いや、まだだよ。
W：じゃあ、いつやるつもり？
M：皿を洗い終わったらやるよ。

㉕ be out in the open：明るみに出る

▶活用例
W : Have you heard the latest about the mayor's scandal?
M : No, what happened?
W : Well, he admitted to taking a bribe.
M : I knew it! Well, at least it's out in the open now.

W：市長のスキャンダルの最新情報をもう聞いた？
M：ううん。何があったの？
W：えーとね、彼は賄賂を受け取ったことを認めたのよ。
M：やっぱりね！　まあ、これで少なくとも公になったってことだね。

*admit to − ing：−したことを認める
*I knew it!：やっぱり！　それ見たことか！

㉖ take it back：取り消す

▶活用例
M : I'm sorry about what I said yesterday.
W : Yeah, well, don't worry about it.
M : No, I feel bad. I wish I could take it back.

M：昨日言ったこと、ごめんね。
W：うん、まあ、気にしないで。
M：いや、後悔しているんだ。取り消せたらいいのに。

*feel bad：後悔する、気がとがめる

㉗ kill 〜：〜にひどい苦痛を与える

▶活用例
W : Are you OK?
M : Yeah, but my back is killing me.
W : Why? What did you do?
M : I was helping my friend move all day yesterday.

W：大丈夫？
M：うん、でも背中が痛くてたまらないんだ。
W：なんで？　何したの？
M：昨日、一日中友達の引越しを手伝っていたから。

 Head Over Heels

㉘ worth a try：試すだけの価値がある

▶活用例
W : My TV's gone haywire.
M : You want me to take a look at it?
W : Can you fix it?
M : I don't know. But it's worth a try.

W：うちのテレビ、おかしくなっちゃった。
M：みてあげようか？
W：直せるの？
M：わかんないけど。でも試す価値はあるよ。

*go haywire：おかしくなる、狂う
*take a look at 〜：〜を見る

㉙ something along the lines of：〜のようなこと

▶活用例
M : What kind of decorations do you want for the party?
W : Well, I haven't really thought about it. Any ideas?
M : Um, I was thinking about something along the lines of 1960's style.
W : That's not a bad idea.

M：パーティの飾り付けはどんなのがいい？
W：うーん、まだあんまり考えてなかったわ。何かアイデアある？
M：そうだねぇ、1960年代風なのはどうかなって思っていたんだけど。
W：悪くないわね。

㉚ Why don't we － ?：－しませんか？

▶活用例
M : Where do you want to go for dinner tonight?
W : I'm kind of in the mood for Italian food.
M : Well, then why don't we go to that new restaurant I told you about?
W : Oh! That sounds great!

M：今夜はどこに夕食を食べに行きたい？
W：どちらかといえば、イタリアンを食べたい気分だわ。
M：よし、じゃあ僕が話したあの新しいレストランに行かない？
W：あー、いいわね！

*be in the mood for 〜：〜を食べたい気分だ、〜をしたい気分だ

▶ SONG #2
I Want...

▶ SONG #2

I Want...

(Verse 1)
I want a fatter paycheck.
I wanna have more time.
I want to hear you tell me,
"I want you to be mine."

I want another cigarette,
But my pack has run dry.
Sometimes I wanna kick ass,
And then I don't even wanna try.

I need a glass of water.
I need something to eat.
I need to take a break.
I really need to get some sleep.

(Pre-Chorus)
There are some things that we want.
There are some things that we need.
Sometimes I don't know which is which.
There's such a fine line in between.

(Chorus)
And right now, right now, right now,
what's making me lose my shit,
The thing that's got me freaking out,
Is something that came out of the blue.
What I'm really, really jonesing for,
really, really dying for is you.

(Verse 2)
I've got to put my feet up.
I've got to take it slow.
I've got to get out of here.
But I've got nowhere to go.

I've gotta cut down on my drinking.
Gotta cut down on the smokes.
Gotta get my shit together.
I'm losing it. No joke.

I wanna come and see you.
Sorry, I take that back.
It's not just that I want to.
I need you before I crack.

(Pre-chorus)

(Chorus)

(Verse 3)
I don't wanna go to work today.
Don't wanna do anything at all.
I'd rather just lounge around.
Maybe later I'll get on the ball.

I'd like to accomplish something.
I'd like to get something done.
I wanna make something of myself.
I feel like such a bum.

I've gotta do something about this.
Gotta get it off my chest.
Gotta lay it out for you,
Because right now I'm such a mess.

(Pre-chorus)

(Chorus)

(Chorus)

(Verse 1)
もっとたくさん給料が欲しい
もっと時間が欲しい
君が僕にこう言うのを聞きたい
「私のものになって欲しいの」

もう一本タバコが欲しい
でももう空っぽ
時々　すごいことをしたくなる
でも　何もしたくない時もある

一杯の水が必要だ
食べ物が必要だ
休みが必要だ
眠ることが必要だ

(Pre-Chorus)
欲しいものがあり
必要なものがある
時々　どっちがどっちだかわからなくなる
二つは紙一重だから

(Chorus)
そして今　まさに今
僕をおかしくさせているもの
僕をパニックに陥れるもの
それは不意にやってきた
僕が本当に欲しいもの
本当に本当にたまらなく欲しいもの　それは君

(Verse 2)
足を放り出して休まなきゃ
ゆっくりしなくちゃ
ここを出なくっちゃ
でもどこにも行く所がないんだ

お酒を減らさなきゃ
タバコも減らさなきゃ
もっとしっかりしなきゃ
もうおかしくなりそうだ　冗談じゃない

君に会いに行きたいよ
ごめん　今のは撤回する
ただ単に会いたいってわけじゃない
僕が壊れてしまう前に君が必要なんだ

(Pre-chorus)

(Chorus)

(Verse 3)
今日は仕事に行きたくない
何もしたくないんだ
だらだらしているほうがいい
たぶん後できちんとやるから

何かを成し遂げたい
何かを仕上げたい
頑張って成功したい
今はほんとに駄目な奴だとしか思えないけど

何かしなくちゃいけないんだ
胸の内を明かさなきゃ
全部君に話さなきゃ
だって僕は今　本当にどうしようもないから

(Pre-chorus)

(Chorus)

(Chorus)

SONG #2　I Want…

曲解説

　1曲目の最後で主人公は告白を決意したものの、そう簡単に告白することはできません。あれこれ思い悩むうちに、恋する幸福感から、次第に狂気じみた様相を呈し始めます。

　人生には「欲しい」物 (**I want a fatter paycheck. I wanna have more time.**) と「必要な」物 (**I need a glass of water. I need something to eat.**) があり、冷静に考えれば、「欲しい」物よりも「必要な」物の方が生きていく上で大切なわけなのですが、「欲しい」気持ちがあまりに高まるとその重要度が増し、どちらがどちらだか分からなくなってしまう (**Sometimes I don't know which is which.**) というのが、この曲のテーマです。

　そして何よりも主人公にそうした気持ちを抱かせているのが彼女の存在であり、それが主人公の心を掻き乱します (**And right now, right now, right now, what's making me lose my shit, the thing that's got me freaking out, is something that came out of the blue. What I'm really, really jonesing for, really, really dying for is you.**)。

　自分がどんどんダメになっていくのを感じ (**I'm losing it. No joke.**)、完全におかしくなる前に彼女が必要だという結論に達します (**I need you before I crack.**)。

　そして、もう一度告白する決意を固めるのです (**I've got to do something about this. Gotta get it off my chest. Gotta lay it out for you because right now I'm such a mess.**)。

　この曲では、ジェフの歌い方も1曲目の宙に浮かぶようなフワフワした柔らかい歌い方から、欲求不満に陥った男の心の叫びを表現する激しいものに変わっています。

　また途中に出てくるオルガンソロも、主人公の狂気を表現するかのように効果的に用いられています。このソロはコンピューターでプログラムされたものであり、一人で一度に弾くことはできません。

I. 学習用歌詞

(Verse 1)
I want a **fatter paycheck**.
　　　　　1
I wanna have more time.
　A
I want to hear you tell me, "I want you to be mine."
　　　　　B

I want another cigarette, but my pack has **run dry**.
　　　　　　　　　　　　　　　　　　　　　2
Sometimes I wanna **kick ass**, and then I don't even wanna try.
　　　　　　　　　　3

I need a glass of water.
I need something to eat.
I need to **take a break**.
　　　　　4
I really need to **get some sleep**.
　　　　　　　　5

(Pre-Chorus)
There are some things that we want.
There are some things that we need.
Sometimes I don't know **which is which**.
　　　　　　　　　　　　6
There's such a fine line in between.
　　　　　　　C

(Chorus)
And right now, right now, right now, what's making me **lose my shit**, the thing that's
　　　　　　　　　　　　　　　D　　　　　　7　　　　　　　E
got me freaking out, is something that came **out of the blue**.
　　　　　　　　　　　　　　　　　　　　　　8
What I'm really, really **jonesing for**, really, really dying for is you.
　　　　　　　　　　9

(Verse 2)
I**'ve got to put my feet up**.
　10　　　4
I've got to **take it slow**.
　　　　　5

▶ SONG #2   I Want…

I've got to **get out of** here.
          11
But I**'ve got nowhere to go**.
       12

I've gotta **cut down on** my drinking.
            13
Gotta cut down on the smokes.
Gotta **get my shit together**.
       14
I'm **losing it**.
     15
No joke.
16

I wanna come and see you.
Sorry, I take that back.
It's not just that I want to.
18   F
I need you before I **crack**.
                     15

(Pre-chorus)

(Chorus)

(Verse 3)
I don't wanna go to work today.
Don't wanna do anything at all.
I'd rather just **lounge around**.
               18
Maybe later I'll **get on the ball**.
                 14

I'd like to accomplish something.
I'd like to get something done.
              G
I wanna **make something of myself**.
         19
I feel like such a bum.
         H

I've gotta **do something about** this.
　　　　　20
Gotta **get it off my chest**.
　　　21
Gotta **lay it out for** you because right now I'm such a **mess**.
　　　21　　　　　　　　　　　　　　　　　15

(Pre-chorus)

(Chorus)

(Chorus)

▶ SONG #2　I Want…

Ⅱ. 語句解説

A. wanna
　wanna ＝ want to は自分のやりたいことを直接的により強く訴えているニュアンスがあります。丁寧に礼儀正しく自分の願望を表現したい時は、would like to を用いた方がいいでしょう。

B. hear you tell
　この hear は知覚動詞と呼ばれるもので、〈hear ～ －〉という形で、「～が－するのを聞く」という意味になります。hear の他に see、watch、feel、notice なども知覚動詞としての用法を持っています。

C. fine
　この fine は「素晴らしい」という意味ではなく、「細い」という意味です。日本人が通常知っている意味と大きく異なる意味を持つ語には注意が必要です。

D. what's making me lose my shit
　この what は先行詞を含む関係代名詞で、the thing(s) which に置き換えられます。また、ここでの make は使役動詞で、〈make ～ －〉で「～に－させる」という意味になります。lose one's shit は「気がおかしくなる」という意味の熟語で、全部をまとめると「私の気をおかしくさせているもの」という意味になり、文の主部になっています。

E. the thing that's got me freaking out
　that's は that has の短縮形です。that は関係代名詞で、that 以下が thing を修飾しています。また、has got は has と同じで、ここでは〈have ～ －ing〉という形になっており、基本的には「～を－している状態にしておく」という意味で、「使役」や「容認」を表します。この部分全体を訳すと、「私をパニック状態に陥れているもの」ということになります。

F. want to
　この want to の後ろには come and see you が省略されています。

G. get something done

〈get 〜 done〉で「〜をやり終える」という意味になります。ここでは〈finish doing 〜〉と同じ意味です。

H. such a bum

〈such a 〜〉で「大変な〜」という意味になることがあり、such a bum で「本当に駄目な奴」という意味になっています。

▶SONG #2 I Want…

III. 重要表現

① fat paycheck：多額の給料

▶活用例
W : You don't seem to like Mark very much.
M : Oh, I'm just jealous.
W : Why?
M : Just because he gets a fatter paycheck than me.

W：あなたはあまりマークが好きじゃないみたいね。
M：あー、ただ羨ましいだけだよ。
W：なんで？
M：ただ単に、彼が僕より給料を多くもらっているからなんだけど。

*seem to ―：―するようだ

② run dry：空になる、なくなる

▶活用例
W : I've gotta run to the store.
M : What do you need?
W : Our alcohol supply has run dry.
M : Oh no! Really? I'll go with you!

W：お店に行かなくちゃ。
M：何が必要なの？
W：お酒がなくなっちゃったのよ。
M：え、うそ！　ほんとに？　僕も一緒に行くよ！

③ kick ass：【卑】凄いことをする、迫力満点だ、徹底的に楽しむ

▶活用例
W : Did you have a good time at the concert?
M : Oh man, it was phenomenal!
W : Yeah, they're pretty good, huh?
M : Oh yeah! They kick ass!

W：コンサート楽しかった？
M：そりゃもう、素晴らしかったよ！
W：だよね。彼らは相当いいでしょ。
M：そうなんだ！　半端じゃないよ！

*～ , huh?：～でしょ？

④ take a break：一休みする
put one's feet up：（座って）休む、リラックスする

▶活用例
W : Man, am I tired!
M : Me, too. You wanna get some coffee?
W : Yeah, I need to put my feet up for a minute, too.
M : Well then, let's take a break.

W：あー、疲れた！
M：僕も！　コーヒーでも飲む？
W：うん、それから、ちょっとの間、座って休みたいわ。
M：だったら、一休みしよう。

⑤ get some sleep：眠る
take it slow：のんきにやる、リラックスする

▶活用例
W : You've been busy lately, huh?
M : Yeah, been working like 27 hours a day.
W : You should take it slow, you know?
M : Yeah, I know. I really need to get some sleep.

W：最近忙しいんでしょ？
M：うん、1日27時間ぐらい働いている感じだよ。
W：もうちょっとのんびりやったほうがいいわよ。わかっているでしょ？
M：うん、わかってる。ほんとに睡眠を取る必要があるんだ。

*like：だいたい

⑥ which is which：どっちがどっちか

▶活用例
M : Do you wanna see a picture of my kids?
W : Sure! I'd love to!
M : This one is Mika and this one is Miki.
W : Wow! Are they identical twins?
M : Yep. That's right.
W : They're so cute! But, I can't tell which is which!

M：僕の子供の写真、見たい？
W：もちろん見たいわ！
M：こっちがミカでこっちがミキ。
W：わー！　2人は一卵性双生児なの？
M：うん、その通り。
W：ほんとに可愛いわねぇー！　でも、どっちがどっちかわからないわ！

▶SONG #2　I Want…

*would love to ー：ぜひーしたい
*can't tell：わからない

⑦ lose one's shit：【卑】頭がおかしくなる

▶活用例
W : Guess who I met in a restaurant last night?
M : Who?
W : Brad Pitt!
M : No way! Did you talk to him?
W : No! I was so excited that I completely lost my shit. And I couldn't say a word!

W：昨日の晩、レストランで誰を見たと思う？
M：誰？
W：ブラッド・ピットよ！
M：まさか！　話しかけた？
W：ううん！　すごい興奮してたから、完全に頭がおかしくなってたの。それで、一言も言えなかったわ！

⑧ out of the blue：突然

▶活用例
M : I just heard they're restructuring our department.
W : Really? What's gonna happen?
M : Some people will probably get cut loose.
W : Oh no! It's scary to think we could just lose our jobs out of the blue like that.

M：今聞いたんだけど、彼らはこの課を再編するらしいよ。
W：ほんとに？　じゃあ、どうなっちゃうの？
M：多分、リストラされる人もいるだろうね。
W：なんですって！　そんなふうに突然仕事を失うかもって考えるだけで怖いわ。

*get cut loose：リストラされる

⑨ jones for 〜：〜が欲しくてたまらない、〜したくてたまらない

▶活用例
M : I'm completely freaking out!
W : Why? What's wrong with you?
M : I'm just really, really jonesing for a smoke. I want one so bad!
W : Oh, I forgot. You're trying to quit. It's pretty tough, huh?

M：僕は完全に気がおかしくなっているよ！

W：なんで？ どうしたの？
M：ほんとにほんとにタバコが吸いたくて仕方がないんだよ。一本欲しくてしょうがないんだ！
W：あー、忘れていた。やめようとしているところなのよね。結構大変なんでしょうね？

*freak out：パニックに陥る、気がおかしくなる
*What's wrong with you?：どうしたの？
*bad：ひどく

⑩ have got to ー：ーしなければならない

▶活用例
M : Do you know what time it is?
W : Yeah, it's 6:29.
M : Oh no! I've got to go right now!
W : Why? What's wrong?
M : I've got to meet my client in one minute!

M：何時だかわかる？
W：うん、6時29分よ。
M：しまった！ すぐに行かなくちゃ！
W：なんで？ どうしたの？
M：1分後に顧客と会わなきゃなんだ！

*Oh, no!：しまった！

⑪ get out of 〜：〜から出る

▶活用例
W : Hey, what time is it?
M : Um, about 4:30.
W : The trains are almost running, huh?
M : Yeah, I think so. You wanna get out of here?
W : Yeah, I'm bushed.

W：ねぇ、今何時？
M：うーんと、4時半ぐらい。
W：もう少しで電車が動き出すわよね？
M：うん、だと思うよ。ここから出たい？
W：うん、もうへとへと。

*be bushed：へとへとに疲れている

▶ SONG #2　I Want…

⑫ have got nowhere to go：行く所がない

▶活用例
W：Hey Jeff. This is Amy. Sorry it's late.
M：No problem. What's up?
W：I just missed my last train and I've got nowhere to go. Any chance I could crash at yours?
M：Again? Ha! Yeah, it's cool. Come on over.

　W：ジェフ。エイミーだけど。ごめんね、夜遅くに。
　M：大丈夫だよ。どうしたの？
　W：最終列車を逃しちゃって、行く所がないの。あなたの所に泊めてもらえたりはしないかしら？
　M：また？　はは！　うん、いいよ。おいでよ。

　*crash at 〜：〜に急に泊めてもらう
　*Any chance SV ？：S が V する可能性はありますか？

⑬ cut down on 〜：〜を減らす

▶活用例
M：Gack! Hrrragh! (coughing)
W：Hey, you OK?
M：Yeah, I've just been smoking too much.
W：You really should cut down on the smokes.

　M：ゲホッ！　ゲホッ！（咳き込む音）
　W：ねぇ、大丈夫？
　M：うん、ちょっと最近タバコ吸い過ぎなんだよね。
　W：本当にタバコは減らしたほうがいいわよ。

⑭ get one's shit together【卑】：きちんとやる、元のしっかりした自分に戻る
　get on the ball：きちんとやる、気をひきしめる

▶活用例
M：I'm so disorganized! I need to get on the ball!
W：What do you mean?
M：Oh, I've just got so much to do. I've really gotta get my shit together.

　M：僕ってほんとにでたらめだなあ！　もっときちんとやらなくちゃ！
　W：どういうこと？
　M：あー、ただやらなくちゃいけないことがたくさんあって。ほんとに、しっかりやらなきゃなんだ。

⑮ **lose it**：自制心を失う、キレる、おかしくなる
　crack：神経がおかしくなる、だめになる
　mess：混乱、滅茶苦茶な様子、滅茶苦茶な人

▶活用例
W : Hey, Jeff. You seem a little freaked out.
M : Yeah, my life's just kind of a mess at the moment.
W : You all right?
M : I dunno. I think I'm losing it. I might crack.

W：ねぇ、ジェフ。ちょっとパニクってるみたいだけど。
M：うん、今ちょっと僕の人生が滅茶苦茶なことになってて。
W：大丈夫？
M：わかんない。自制心を失いつつあるみたい。頭がおかしくなるかも。

⑯ **No joke.**：冗談じゃない

▶活用例
M : Hey, did you hear that someone wrote "gullible" all over my ceiling?
W : No way! Are you serious?
M : No joke.
W : Wait, I don't see it. Where did they write it?
M : Ha! Sorry. I was just messing with you.

M：ねぇ、僕の部屋の天井いっぱいに、誰かが「のろま」って書いたってこと聞いた？
W：うそでしょ！　マジ？
M：冗談じゃないよ。
W：待って、私には見えないわ。どこに書いたって？
M：はは！　ごめん。ちょっとからかってみただけ。

*mess with 〜：〜をからかう

SONG #2　I Want…

⑰ It's not just that S V.：ただ S が V するということだけではない

▶活用例

W : Why didn't you come to karaoke with us last night?
M : Oh, I was kind of tired.
W : But you love karaoke!
M : Well, it's not just that I was tired. I can't stand listening to Jeff sing. He's terrible!

W：昨日の晩、なんで私達と一緒にカラオケに行かなかったの？
M：あー、ちょっと疲れていたんだ。
W：でも、あなたカラオケ大好きじゃない！
M：うん、ただ疲れていただけじゃないんだ。ジェフが歌うのを聞くのが耐えられないんだよ。彼、ひどいから！

*stand：我慢する
*listen to 〜 ー：〜がーするのを聞く

⑱ lounge around：ダラダラ過ごす

▶活用例

W : Are you working today?
M : No, I finally got a day off.
W : Oh yeah? What are you up to?
M : Nothing. Just lounging around.

W：今日は仕事？
M：ううん、やっと一日休みが取れたんだよ。
W：あぁ、そうなんだ？　何するの？
M：なーんにも。ただダラダラしてるだけ。

*get 〜 off：〜休みを取る
*be up to 〜：〜をする、〜しようと計画する

⑲ make something of oneself：頑張って成功する、立身出世する

▶活用例

W : Did you hear? Jeff just got a record contract!
M : No way! How'd he do that?
W : Apparently, he just went in for an audition and that was it.
M : That's so cool! He's finally gonna make something of himself.

W：聞いた？　ジェフがレコードの契約を取りつけたって！
M：うそだろ！　どうやって？
W：どうやらね、オーディションに行ってそうなったみたいよ。
M：すっげー！　彼もついに出世するのかぁ。

⑳ **do something about ～**：～をどうにかする

▶活用例
W : Looks like Simon's causing trouble again.
M : Oh, what's he doing now?
W : I think he's trying to start a fight with the waiter.
M : Again? All right. Hold on a second. I'll do something about it.

W：サイモンがまた問題起こしちゃっているみたいよ。
M：あぁ、彼はいま何してるの？
W：多分、あのウェイターと喧嘩を始めようとしているんじゃない？
M：また？　わかったよ。ちょっと待って。どうにかしてくるから。

***Looks like S V.**：**S** は **V** するようだ
***hold on**：待つ

㉑ **get it off one's chest**：心の内を明かす
　lay it out for ～：～に細かく話す

▶活用例
M : Amy, is something bugging you?
W : Yeah, but I don't wanna talk about it.
M : Come on. You can tell me. Go on and get it off your chest.
W : All right. I'll lay it out for you.

M：エイミー、何かいらいらすることでもあるの？
W：うん、でも話したくないの。
M：さぁ、言ってみなよ。打ち明けてみて。
W：わかった。あなたに細かく話すわ。

***bug**：いらいらさせる
***Go on and ‐ .**：どうぞ‐してください

▶ SONG #3
Fall Into Place

▶ SONG #3
Fall Into Place

(Verse 1)
Today is the most beautiful day.
I feel like I'm a thousand miles away,
From the hustle and bustle of big city life.
I'm in my own little world and I mean it, it's nice.

For once I got up on the right side of the bed.
Got more than enough sleep and cleared my head.
Had a couple cups of coffee while checking my mail.
Got one from a friend who I hadn't heard from in a while.

(Chorus)
And I say…
There are some days when things just fall into place.
When all of your troubles vanish without a trace.
And you, you find yourself staring out into space,
Feeling as good as can be,
Everything has clicked perfectly.
And it's hard to wipe the smile off of your face.

(Verse 2)
I left this morning with time to spare.
Got stuck in some traffic, but I didn't really care.
If you had asked me, "Hey, what's on your mind?"
I'd probably smile and say, "Well, not the daily grind."

Got to work early enough to grab a cuppa joe.
Had a peek at the paper. Nothing I didn't know.
Got a bit of work done at my own pace.
Then finally at lunch time, I caught a glimpse of your face.

(Bridge)
You walked into the deli where I was grabbing a bite.
You looked better than usual, completely out of sight.
You sat down next to me at the table to my right.
I was totally nervous. I was on the verge of fright.
You turned to me and asked, "Are you alright?"
I smiled and said, "I'm fine. By the way, by the way, are you busy tonight?"

(Verse 3)
After work, I cleaned myself up.
Scrounged up some coffee, finished off another cup.
Went downstairs to wait for you.
And then you showed up, and suddenly I knew,

Not only was it a beautiful day,
But the evening also would be this way.
We had dinner and a glass of wine.
And it became obvious you were meant to be mine.

(Chorus)

(Chorus)

(Verse 1)
今日は最高の日だ
千マイルも彼方にいる気分
都会の喧騒からは
自分だけの小さな世界の中　ほんと　気持ちいい

今日ばかりは朝からごきげん
十分な睡眠で　頭もすっきり
メールをチェックしながら　コーヒーを２，３杯
メールの一つは　しばらく音沙汰のなかった友達からだった

(Chorus)
そして僕は言う・・・
すべてがうまくいく日もある
すべての問題が跡形もなく消える日
気がつくと宙を見つめている
この上なくいい気分で
すべてが完全にうまくいく
そう　笑顔が簡単に消えることはない

(Verse 2)
今朝は余裕をもって家を出た
渋滞にはまったけど　そんなことはお構いなし
「ねぇ　何考えてるの？」って聞かれたら
多分笑顔でこう言うだろう　「お決まりの日課以外のことさ」

コーヒーを一杯飲めるくらい余裕で会社に着いて
新聞をながめたけど　知らないことは何一つ無い
自分のペースで仕事を軽くこなす
そしてやっとランチタイム　君の顔を少しだけ見られた

(Bridge)
食事をしていたデリに君も入ってきた
君はいつもより美しい　完璧な美しさ
君が僕の右隣のテーブルに座ると
僕はめちゃくちゃ緊張して　心臓がドキドキ
君はこっちを向いて聞いた「大丈夫？」
僕は笑って言う「大丈夫だよ　ところで今夜忙しい？」

(Verse 3)
仕事の後　僕は身なりを整える
コーヒーを手に入れて　ぐっと飲みほした
一階に行き　君を待つ僕
そして　君が姿を見せたとき　突然僕にはわかったんだ

昼間だけじゃなく
夜も素晴らしいものになるということを
僕達は夕食をとり、ワインを楽しむ
そしてはっきりとわかったのは　君が僕のものになる運命にあるということ

(Chorus)

(Chorus)

▶ SONG #3　Fall Into Place

曲解説

　ゆったりとしたリズムに乗って、ギターとストリングスが広がりのある音空間を表現する中、主人公は、今日は最高の日だ（**Today is the most beautiful day.**）と歌い始めます。2曲目における狂気を切り抜けて、この曲では、主人公は落ち着きを取り戻しているのです。

　十分な睡眠で頭もすっきり（**Got more than enough sleep and cleared my head.**）。全てがうまく行き、問題も解決します（**There are some days when things just fall into place. When all of your troubles vanish without a trace.**）。

　そしてついに、昼食時にデリで彼女が自分の隣に座ると、彼女のあまりの美しさに緊張しながらも、彼女をデートに誘います（**You walked into the deli where I was grabbing a bite. You looked better than usual, completely out of sight. You sat down next to me at the table to my right. I was totally nervous. I was on the verge of fright. You turned to me and asked, "Are you alright?" I smiled and said, "I'm fine. By the way, by the way, are you busy tonight?"**）。

　その夜、彼女と一緒に食事とワインを楽しんだ主人公は、彼女が自分のものになる運命にあると直感的に感じるのです（**We had dinner and a glass of wine.And it became obvious you were meant to be mine.**）。

　この曲では脚韻が多用されています。脚韻とは、詩や歌詞において、その各行の最後の部分に同じ音が用いられていることを言いますが、アメリカやイギリスのポップスではよく見られるものです。脚韻を踏むためには、意味の流れを自然に保ったまま、各行の最後に、語尾に同じ発音を持つ語をもってこなければならないため、作者にとっては非常に難しい作業となります。しかし、ジェフはこの曲において、見事に脚韻を踏んでいます。歌詞の各行の最後の語に注目し、同じ音が用いられている部分を確認してみてください（スペースの関係で、歌詞の1行が2行にわかれている場合もあります。コンマやピリオドの直前の語に注目してください）。

I．学習用歌詞

(Verse 1)
Today is the most beautiful day.
　　　　　　　　　A

I **feel like** I'm a thousand miles away from the **hustle and bustle** of big city life.
　1　　　　　　　　　　　　　　　　　　　　　　2

I**'m in my own little world** and I **mean it**, it's nice.
　3　　　　　　　　　　　　　B 4

For once I **got up on the right side of the bed**.
5　　　　　6

Got **more than enough** sleep and **cleared my head**.
　　　5　　　　　　　　　　　　7

Had a couple cups of coffee while checking my mail.
Got one from a friend who I hadn't heard from in a while.
C

(Chorus)
And I say, there are some days when things just **fall into place**.
　　　　　　　　　　D　　　　　　　　　　　　　　8

When all of your troubles **vanish without a trace**.
E　　　　　　　　　　　9

And you, you find yourself **staring out into space**, feeling **as** good **as can be**.
　　　　　　　　F　　　　10　　　　　　　　　G　　　　11

Everything has **clicked** perfectly.
　　　　　　　　8

And it's hard to **wipe the smile off of your face**.
　　　　　　　H　　　12

(Verse 2)
I left this morning with **time to spare**.
　　　　　　　　　　　　13

Got stuck in some traffic, but I didn't really care.
14

If you had asked me, "Hey, what**'s on your mind**?" I'd probably smile and say,
I　　　　　　　　　　　10

"Well, not the **daily grind**."
　　　　　　　2

Got to work early enough to **grab a cuppa joe**.
　　　　　　　　　　　　15　　J　　K

Had a peek at the paper.
Nothing I didn't know.
L

SONG #3 Fall Into Place

Got a bit of work done **at my own pace**.
M   16

Then finally at lunch time, I **caught a glimpse of** your face.
         17

(Bridge)
You walked into the deli where I was **grabbing a bite**.
    N   15

You looked better than usual, completely **out of sight**.
         18

You sat down next to me at the table to my right.
I was totally nervous.
I **was on the verge of** fright.
 19

You turned to me and asked, "Are you alright?"
I smiled and said, "I'm fine. By the way, by the way, are you busy tonight?"

(Verse 3)
After work, I **cleaned myself up**.
    20

Scrounged up some coffee, **finished off** another cup.
20   21   O

Went downstairs to wait for you.
And then you showed up, and suddenly I knew not only was it a beautiful day, but
              P

the evening also would be this way.
    P

We had dinner and a glass of wine.
And it became obvious you **were meant to** be mine.
 Q   22

(Chorus)

(Chorus)

II. 語句解説

A. beautiful
　beautiful は、「天気がいい」という意味でよく用いられますが、ここでは「素晴らしい」という意味で用いられています。

B. mean it
　mean it は「本気である、本気で言っている」という意味ですが、何を本気で言っているかというと、次の it's nice ということを本気で言っているというわけです。したがって、「『自分だけの小さな世界の中にいるのは、素晴らしいことだ』ということを、本気で言っている」という意味になります。

C. Got one from a friend who I hadn't heard from in a while.
　この who は関係代名詞で、who 以下が直前の friend を修飾しています。「友達」、どういう友達かと言うと、「しばらく便りがなかった」友達ということです。

　who の後ろを見ると、I hadn't heard from in a while となっており、from の後ろにあるべき him/her が接続詞の働きも兼ねて関係代名詞 who に姿を変えて I の前に出たわけです。ですから目的格である him/her の代わりなので、本来なら関係代名詞も目的格の whom が用いられるべきところですが、現代英語では whom はあまり用いられず、who となる場合が多く見られます。

　また、hadn't heard は〈had+p.p.〉で過去完了です。ここでは、述語動詞 got よりも hear という動作の方が時間的により前の動作であることを示しています。

D. some days when things just fall into place
　この when は関係副詞で、when 以下が直前の days を修飾しています。「日」、どういう日かと言うと、「物事が上手く行く」日ということです。

E. When
　この when も D の when と用法は全く同じです。この when の前には There are some days が省略されています。

F. find yourself staring
　ここでの find は第5文型〈SVOC〉を作っています。ここでは C に現在分詞 (ing 形) が来ており、〈find 〜 − ing〉で「〜が−しているのに気付く」という意味になっています。

▶ SONG #3　Fall Into Place

G. feeling
　この ing 形は現在分詞で、分詞構文を作っています。分詞構文は主節内の動詞を修飾する副詞句として働きます。「ーする時」、「ーするので」、「ーするけれど」、「ーしながら」等様々な意味を表わしますが、ここでは「ーしながら」の意味となり、star-ing を修飾しています。つまり、「この上なくいい気分で見つめている」ということです。

H. it's hard to wipe
　it は仮主語、to 以下が真主語となっており、〈It is 〜 to ー．〉で、「ーすることは〜だ」という意味になっています。主部（この文の場合は to wipe the smile off of your face）が長くて、述部（この文の場合は is hard）が短い場合に、文のバランスを整えるためであったり、先に自分の考え（この場合は hard）を言うために、このような形が用いられます。

I. If you had asked me, "Hey, what's on your mind?" I'd probably smile
　〈If S1 had p.p., S2 would ー．〉は仮定法で、「もし S1 が（過去に）〜したとしたら、S2 は（現在）ーするだろう」という意味になります。この歌詞では、全体が過去の話として過去形で書かれており、I'd probably smile の部分も I'd probably have smiled という形にして、「おそらく笑ったであろう」というように、過去の話として統一するほうが筋が通ります。その辺りの時間の表現に混乱が見られますが、こうした混乱は日常会話ではしばしば見られるものです。

J. cuppa
　cuppa は cup of のことで、実際の発音通りに綴られたものです。

K. joe
　この joe は coffee のことですが、標準的な英語というわけではありません。ここでは、後に出てくる know と韻を踏むようにするために、わざと用いられています。

L. Nothing I didn't know.
Nothing の前に There was という語句が省略されています。

M. Got a bit of work done

〈get 〜 p.p.〉は「〜が―された状態にする」というのが基本的な意味です。ここでは、「少しの仕事がなされた状態にする」ということで、「仕事を少し終わらせる」という意味になります。

N. the deli where I was grabbing a bite

この where は関係副詞で、where 以下が直前の deli を修飾しています。「デリ」、どういうデリかというと、「僕が軽く食事をしていた」デリということです。

関係副詞を含む文が出てきた場合、関係副詞を〈接続詞＋副詞 (where の場合は there)〉に置き換えて、前から後ろに意味を取る形で処理するとスムーズに解釈できます。You walked into the deli where I was grabbing a bite. という文について言えば、まず deli までを訳し (「君はデリに入ってきた」)、where を and ＋ there に置き換えて、「それで、そこでは僕が食事をしてたんだけど」と考えるわけです。

O. another

朝、職場に着いて飲んだコーヒーに続いて、2 回目のコーヒーということで another が使われています。

P. was, would

主節の動詞が knew と過去形であるため、従属節内の動詞・助動詞も was、would と過去形になっています。時制の一致と呼ばれるものです。

Q. it

この it は仮主語で、you were meant to be mine が真主語です。「君が僕のものになる運命である」ということが「明らかになった」ということです。本来は you の前に名詞節を作る that が入りますが、ここでは省略されています。

▶ SONG #3 Fall Into Place

III. 重要表現

① S feel like S V.：S は V するように感じる

▶活用例
M : Man, it's so hot today!
W : I know! It's unbearable!
M : It must be over 40 degrees.
W : Yeah, and so humid, too! I feel like I'm in a sauna!

M：うわぁ、今日はすごく暑いなあ！
W：そうね！ 耐えられないわ！
M：40°以上あるに違いないね。
W：ええ、それに、すごい蒸し蒸しするわね！ サウナの中にいるみたい！

***Man.**：うわぁ

② hustle and bustle：喧騒
daily grind：日課

▶活用例
W : The daily grind is really wearing me out.
M : Yeah, it can get to you, huh?
W : It's just all this hustle and bustle day in and day out.
M : Yeah, I know what you mean.

W：日課をこなすんで、ほんとにへとへとなんだけど。
M：うん、こたえるよね。
W：全ては、この毎日の喧騒なのよね。
M：うん、君の言いたいことわかるよ。

***wear 〜 out**：〜を疲れさせる
***day in and day out**：毎日毎日
***I know what you mean.**：君の言いたいことわかるよ

③ be in one's own little world：自分だけの小さな世界の中にいる

▶活用例
W : Have you talked to Jeff recently?
M : Yeah, he's acting a little odd.
W : You think he's OK?
M : I'm sure he's fine. He's just in his own little world.

W：最近ジェフと話した？
M：うん、なんだかちょっと行動が奇妙なんだよね。
W：彼、大丈夫だと思う？
M：きっと大丈夫だよ。自分の世界に入っちゃっているだけだから。

④ mean it：本気だ、本気で言っている

▶活用例
W : Yesterday, when you said that you wanted to marry me, did you mean it?
M : Of course! I was serious.
W : Well, you were pretty drunk, you know.
M : Yeah, but still, I meant it.

W：昨日、あなたが私と結婚したいって言った時、本気だったの？
M：もちろんさ！　本気だったよ。
W：うーん、あなた相当酔っていたから。でしょ？
M：うん、それでも本気だったんだよ。

*you know：〜でしょ、ご存知の通り、あのね、えーと

⑤ for once：今度だけは
more than enough 〜：十分過ぎる〜

▶活用例
W : You wanna stay for one more beer?
M : Actually, I've had more than enough alcohol. I think I'm gonna take off pretty soon.
W : Really? For once, I'm drinking more than you!

W：もう一杯ビール付き合わない？
M：実際、十分過ぎるほど飲んじゃって。もうすぐ帰ろうと思っているんだけど。
W：ほんとに？　今度ばかりは、私のほうがあなたより飲んでいるわ！

*take off：すぐに出る

⑥ get up on the right/wrong side of the bed：起きた時から機嫌がいい／悪い

▶活用例
W : What's up with the boss today? He's acting really nasty.
M : I know! But there's nothing going on as far as I know.
W : I guess he just got up on the wrong side of the bed.

W：今日は社長どうしちゃったの？　ほんと意地が悪いんだけど。
M：そうなんだ！　でも、僕の知っている限りでは何もないんだけどね。
W：ただ朝から虫の居所が悪かったのね。

*as far as S V：S が V する限りは

▶ SONG #3   Fall Into Place

⑦ clear one's head：頭をすっきりさせる

▶活用例
M : This project is driving me mad!
W : Well, you've been working on it constantly for three weeks.
M : Yeah, it's getting to me.
W : Why don't you take the rest of the day off? Get some fresh air and clear your head.
M : That's not a bad idea.

M：このプロジェクト、ほんとに頭にくるなあ！
W：そうねぇ、3週間もぶっ続けでこの仕事をしているんだもの。
M：うん、それがこたえているんだよね。
W：今日はこの後、休みを取ったら？　新鮮な空気を吸って、頭をすっきりさせなさいよ。
M：それは悪くないね。

*drive ～ mad：～を怒らせる
*work on ～：～に従事する

⑧ fall into place：上手くいく
click：しっくりいく

▶活用例
M : I can't believe how well that meeting went!
W : Yeah, everything just fell right into place.
M : Yeah. Everything clicked. Just like clockwork.

M：あの会議があんなに上手くいったなんて信じられない！
W：うん、ほんとに全てが上手くいったわね。
M：うん。全てがしっくりきたね。ほんとにきっちりね。

*like clockwork：正確に

⑨ vanish without a trace：跡形もなく消える

▶活用例
W : Have you seen Simon?
M : Not for an hour or so. Where'd he go?
W : I don't know. He just vanished without a trace.
M : Well, he does that sometimes when he's been drinking.

W：サイモン見かけた？
M：一時間くらい前に見たよ。彼、どこに行っちゃったの？
W：わからない。跡形も無く消えちゃったのよ。
M：うーん、飲んでいる時に、時々そういうことをするんだよね。

⑩ stare out into space：宙をじっと見つめる
be on one's mind：気にかかっている、考えている

▶活用例
W : Jeff? Hey, Jeff!
M : Huh? What?
W : You were just staring out into space. What's on your mind?
M : Oh, I was just thinking about Amy.
W : Ah, I should've known.

W：ジェフ？ ねぇ、ジェフ！
M：うーん？ 何？
W：ぼけーっと宙を見つめていたけど、何考えているの？
M：あぁ、ただエイミーのことを考えていたんだ。
W：あー、考えればわかるよね。

*I should have known.：気が付かなかったが当然そうだ

⑪ as 〜 as can be：この上なく〜

▶活用例
W : Finally! A vacation!
M : Yeah, I've been waiting for this for so long!
W : Me, too. And now that it's here, I feel just as good as can be.
M : Same here. Same here.

W：やっと来たわ！ バケーション！
M：うん、これをほんとに長い間待ち続けていたんだよね！
W：私もよ。でもやっとバケーションで、最高の気分。
M：ほんとだね。同感。

*Same here.：全く同感だ

⑫ wipe the smile off of one's face：ニヤニヤ笑いをやめる

▶活用例
W : Jeff, are you thinking about Amy again?
M : Yeah. Why?
W : Well, you should wipe the smile off of your face. The boss is looking at you.
M : Oh, I didn't realize that. Thanks.

W：ジェフ、またエイミーのこと考えているの？
M：うん。何で？
W：うーん、そのにやけた顔をやめなさいよ。上司が見ているわよ。
M：あぁ、気が付かなかった。ありがとう。

SONG #3 Fall Into Place

⑬ time to spare：余った時間、自由に使える時間

▶活用例
W : Have you finished everything for our presentation?
M : Yep, it's all taken care of. We're ready.
W : Great. That didn't take very long.
M : Yeah, it all came together pretty quickly and we've got plenty of time to spare.

W：私達のプレゼンの準備、全部終わった？
M：うん、全部準備済み。いつでも OK だよ。
W：すごい。あまり時間かからなかったわね。
M：うん、結構早くまとめられたから、随分時間が余っているよ。

*come together：まとまる

⑭ get stuck in traffic：渋滞にはまる

▶活用例
W : Hello?
M : Hi, it's me. I'm gonna be about 15 minutes late.
W : OK. Where are you now?
M : Near City Hall, but it's rush hour, and I got stuck in traffic

W：もしもし？
M：やあ、僕だよ。15 分くらい遅れそうなんだけど。
W：わかったわ。今どこ？
M：市役所の近く。でも今ラッシュアワーで、渋滞にはまっちゃったんだ。

⑮ grab a cuppa joe：コーヒーを 1 杯飲む
　grab a bite：軽い食事をする

▶活用例
M : Hey Amy. You wanna grab a bite or a cuppa joe?
W : Actually, I'd rather go out for a beer.
M : Even better. I'll meet you downstairs after work.
W : Sounds good.

M：ねぇ、エイミー。何か軽く食べるか、コーヒーでも飲む？
W：実を言うと、ビールを飲みに行くほうがいいのよね。
M：そのほうがずっといいね。仕事が終わったら下の階で会おう。
W：いいわよ。

⑯ at one's own pace：〜自身のペースで

▶活用例
W : You're not finished yet?
M : No. I'm going at my own pace.
W : Well, your pace is too slow. Hurry up!
M : OK. Sorry, boss.

W：まだ終わってないの？
M：はい。自分のペースでやっているものですから。
W：うーん、あなたのペースはちょっと遅過ぎるわね。急いで！
M：わかりました。すみません、社長。

⑰ catch a glimpse of 〜：〜をちょっと見る

▶活用例
W : Did you hear that our favorite band is going to have an album signing in Shinjuku tomorrow?
M : No way! You gonna go see 'em?
W : Of course! I'll be happy if I can just catch a glimpse of them!
M : Yeah, I may have to call in sick to work.

W：私達の大好きなバンドが、明日新宿でアルバムのサイン会をやるっていうの聞いた？
M：うそだろ！　見に行くの？
W：もちろんよ！　ちょっぴりでも彼らを見られたら嬉しいわ！
M：そうだね、僕も病気で休むって、会社に電話しなくちゃかも。

*go see：見に行く
*call in sick：病欠の電話を入れる

⑱ out of sight：とてつもない、素晴らしい

▶活用例
W : Hey, do you have a picture of Amy?
M : Of course! Here, look.
W : Wow! She's out of sight! You really like her, huh?
M : You can tell?
W : Come on! It's written all over your face!

W：ねぇ、エイミーの写真持っている？
M：もちろんだよ！　ほら、見て。
W：うぁわー！　彼女、すごくきれいね！　あなた、ほんとに彼女のこと好きなのね？
M：わかる？
W：当たり前よ！　顔中にそう書いてあるもん！

*be written all over one's face：顔に書いてある

▶ SONG #3　Fall Into Place

⑲ be on the verge of ～：～寸前だ

> ▶活用例
> W : I'm so nervous about this job interview.
> M : Yeah, you seem a bit on edge.
> W : Actually, I'm on the verge of completely losing it.
> M : Oh, come on. You'll do fine. Don't worry about it.

W：この就職面接のこと考えると、ほんと心配になるわ。
M：うん、ちょっと不安になっているように見えるよ。
W：っていうか、ほんとに頭がおかしくなる寸前なの。
M：おい、何言ってんだよ。大丈夫だよ。心配するなって。

⑳ clean oneself up：身なりを整える
　scrounge up ～：（探し回って）～を手に入れる

> ▶活用例
> W : Whoa, Jeff. What's wrong with you?
> M : I was too hungover this morning to shower or shave.
> W : You know, you really should scrounge up a hairbrush and a razor. You'd better clean yourself up a bit before the boss catches a glimpse of you.
> M : Yeah, thanks. I'll see what I can do.

W：まあ、ジェフ。どうしたの？
M：今朝二日酔いがひどくて、シャワーも髭剃りもできなかったんだ。
W：わかっているとは思うけど、ヘアブラシとかみそり探してきたほうがいいわよ。社長にちらっと見られる前に、少し身ぎれいにしとかないと。
M：うん、ありがとう。なんとかしてみるよ。

*I'll see what I can do.：なんとかしてみるよ、できるだけやってみるよ

㉑ finish off：（飲食物を）平らげる

> ▶活用例
> W : You ready to go?
> M : Yeah, but we shouldn't waste the rest of this whiskey.
> W : You're right. Let's finish off the bottle, then call it a night.
> M : OK. Sounds good to me.

W：出る準備できた？
M：うん、でもこの残りのウィスキーを無駄にしないほうがいいよね。
W：そうね。じゃあ、このボトルを空けたら、今夜はお開きにしましょう。
M：わかった。それでいいよ。

*call it a night：今夜はこれで終わりにする

㉒ be meant to ー：ーするよう運命づけられている

▶活用例

W : You know what Jeff told me yesterday?
M : What did he say?
W : That he wants to marry me.
M : Was he drunk?
W : A little. But today he said he had meant it.
M : Really? Wow. Maybe you two are truly meant to be together!

W：昨日、ジェフが私に何て言ったか知っている？
M：何て言ったの？
W：私と結婚したいって。
M：彼、酔っていたの？
W：少しね。でも今日、それでも本気だったんだって言ってたわ。
M：ほんと？　わー。たぶん、君達二人は本当に一緒になる運命なんだよ！

SONG #4
Nothing You Can Do

▶ SONG #4
Nothing You Can Do

(Verse 1)
Everything was going perfectly,
Not a cloud in the sky.
But things can change so quickly,
In the blink of an eye.

I thought I had a grip on things.
Thought I knew what I should do.
But one little thing slipped by me,
And now I haven't got a clue.

Any way you look at it,
I'm blocked at every turn.
Everything that I have built,
Is about to crash and burn.

(Chorus)
When things are going smoothly,
When you've got it all figured out,
One little thing can happen,
That turns it all around.
And the sky comes crashing down.
And down here on the ground,
There's really nothing you can do.

(Verse 2)
My meetings aren't going so well.
My boss is really stressed.
My performance is dropping.
I'm falling behind the rest.

My job is on the block,
And I'm completely on edge.
Can't seem to pull it off,
Even though I'm giving it my best.

They may have to cut me loose.
They may have to let me go.
It's really getting to me.
I just hope that it doesn't show.

(Chorus)

(Verse 3)
And as if this wasn't bad enough,
It went from bad to worse.
Everything has fallen apart.
I swear I must be cursed.

First my job went down the drain.
Got laid off last night.
As for the girl I've been seeing,
All we do is fight.

I don't know what's happening.
Don't know how much more I can take.
We all get to a certain point,
And then we finally break.

(Chorus)

(Verse 1)
すべてが完璧にうまくいっていた
空に雲ひとつないみたいに
でもすぐに状況は一変してしまう
一瞬の瞬きのうちに

僕は状況をしっかり把握していると思っていた
何をすべきかわかっていると思っていた
でもちょっとしたことを一つ見落としていたんだ
今はどうしていいのかわからない

どう見ても
八方塞がり
僕が作り上げたすべてが
今まさに台無しになろうとしている

(Chorus)
物事がスムーズに進んでいる時
自分がすべてを把握しきっている時に
ほんのひとつの小さなことが起こって
すべてをひっくり返してしまうことがある
そして空が大きな音を立てて崩れ落ちてくる
そうなると、この地上では
もはやできることは何もない

(Verse 2)
会議は不調
上司はストレスにまみれ
僕の成績も下り坂
同僚からは遅れを取るばかり

仕事を失いかけて
完全にナーバスになっている僕
上手く切り抜けられそうもない
全力を尽くしてはいるけれど

会社は僕を切り捨てなければならないのかも
手放さなければならないのかも
僕には、それがほんとにこたえてる
今はただ　それを誰にも気付かれないことを祈るばかりだ

(Chorus)

(Verse 3)
そしてこれだけじゃ苦しみは足りないといわんばかりに
状況はさらに悪化した
今やすべてがバラバラ
断言する　僕は呪われているに違いない

まず最初に仕事が台無しになって
昨夜ついに僕はクビ
付き合っている彼女とは
いつも喧嘩ばかり

何が起きているのかわからない
あとどのぐらい我慢できるのかわからない
一線を越えれば
あとはもう壊れるだけ

(Chorus)

SONG #4 Nothing You Can Do

曲解説

　アコースティックギターから始まる、ゆったりとした曲。気持ちのいい状況を歌った歌かと思いきや、幸せから一転、急に全てがダメになっていく様子を表現している歌です。ですから、この曲のゆったり感というのは、主人公が状況の変化に唖然とし、ある種の放心状態に陥っている姿を表現したものといえます。

　実は、3曲目からこの4曲目の間には、内容的に少し隔たりがあります。3曲目の最後で、主人公が彼女との運命的なものを感じた後、二人は結ばれ、しばし幸せな時を送ります。しかし、その幸せは長くは続かず、急に暗雲が垂れ込めてくるという展開なのです。

　生活の全てをしっかり把握していると思っていたら、ある一つの小さなことを見落としていて、急速に事態は悪化します（**I thought I had a grip on things. Thought I knew what I should do. But one little thing slipped by me and now I haven't got a clue.**）。

　そして、自分の作り上げたものが全て駄目になってしまいそうな状況に陥ります（**Everything that I have built is about to crash and burn.**）。

　仕事もうまくいかず（**My performance is dropping. I'm falling behind the rest.**）、ついにクビ（**First my job went down the drain. Got laid off last night.**）。さらに、彼女とは喧嘩ばかり（**As for the girl I've been seeing, all we do is fight.**）。

　こうした状況の中、主人公は我慢の限界を感じ、自分の頭がおかしくなってしまう可能性を示唆しています。（**Don't know how much more I can take. We all get to a certain point, and then we finally break.**）。

I. 学習用歌詞

(Verse 1)
Everything was going perfectly, <u>not a cloud in the sky</u>.
　　　　　　　　　　　　　　　　　A

But <u>things can change</u> so quickly, **in the blink of an eye**.
　　　B　　　　　　　　　　　　　　1

I thought I **had a grip on** things.
　　　　　　　　2
Thought I knew what I should do.
But one little thing **slipped by** me and now I **haven't got a clue**.
　　　　　　　　　　3

Any way you look at it, I'm **blocked at every turn**.
5　　　　　　　　　　　6
Everything that I have built **is about to crash and burn**.
　　　　　　　　　　　　　7　　　　　　8

(Chorus)
When things are **going smoothly**, when you**'ve got it all figured out**,
　　　　　　　　　9　　　　　　　　　　　　　2
one little thing can happen that **turns** it all **around**.
C　　　　　　　　　　　　　　10
And the sky <u>comes crashing down</u>.
　　　　　　　　D
And down here on the ground, there's really nothing you can do.

(Verse 2)
My meetings aren't going so well.
My boss is really stressed.
My performance is dropping.
I'm **falling behind** the rest.
　　　11　　　　　　E

My job **is on the block**, and I**'m** completely **on edge**.
　　　　12　　　　　　　13
Can't seem to **pull it off** even though I'm **giving it my best**.
　　　　　　　14　　　　F　　　　　　15

They may have to **cut** me **loose**.
G　　　　　　　　16

SONG #4 Nothing You Can Do

They may have to **let** me **go**.
              16
It's really **getting to** me.
           17
I just hope that it doesn't show.
H

(Chorus)

(Verse 3)
And **as if** this wasn't bad enough, it **went from bad to worse**.
     18   19
Everything has **fallen apart**.
               20
I swear I must be cursed.

First my job **went down the drain**.
           21
Got laid off last night.
16
As for the girl I've been **seeing**, all we do is fight.
22   I   23

I don't know what's happening.
Don't know how much more I can take.
We all get to a certain point, and then we finally break.
J   J

(Chorus)

II. 語句解説

A. not a cloud in the sky
　この部分の前に there being という語句が省略されています。その being は現在分詞で、存在を表わす分詞構文を作る時に there being 〜という形が用いられます。

B. things can change
　この can は、「能力」ではなく「可能性」を表わす can です。つまり、「状況は変わることができる」ということではなく、「状況は変わる可能性がある」ということです。

C. one little thing can happen that turns it all around
　この that は関係代名詞で、that 以下が thing を修飾しています。この場合のように、先行詞と関係詞節が離れている場合もあります。

D. comes crashing down
　〈come − ing〉で「−してくる」という意味を表わします。come running 、come flying、come speeding 等も同様です。

E. rest
　rest には「休息」という意味の rest 以外に、「残り」「その他」という意味の rest があり、ここでは後者です。the rest で「その他の人々」という意味になります。

F. even though I'm giving it my best
　even though も even if も「たとえ〜だとしても」と訳されますが、even though の場合は、「実際に〜なのだが」という意味合いであり、even if は「仮に〜だとしても」という意味合いで使われます。ですから、この部分は「実際にベストを尽くしているんだけれども」という意味になります。

G. They
　この They は会社の経営者側、管理職を漠然と指しています。

H. I just hope that it doesn't show.
　この show は「見せる」という意味の他動詞ではなく、「あらわになる」という意味の自動詞です。it は「会社を首になりそうになって弱っている状態」のことを表わして

SONG #4　Nothing You Can Do

いるので、文全体を直訳すると、「会社を首になりそうになって弱っていることが、人の目にわかるようにあらわになっていないことを願っている」という意味になります。

I. I've been seeing

I've は I have の短縮形で、〈have been － ing〉という形は現在完了進行形と呼ばれ、「(現在に至るある期間) ずっと−してきて、今も−している」という意味を表します。ここでの see は「付き合う」という意味ですから、「このところずっと付き合っていて、今でも付き合っている」という意味になります。

J. We, we

この We は主人公と彼女を指しているのではなく、「私達はみんな」ということで、一般化して言うために用いられています。

ここでは、「私達は誰でも、ある点に到達すると、精神的におかしくなってしまう」ということを言っています。

III. 重要表現

① in the blink of an eye：一瞬のうちに

▶活用例
W : Did you know it was going to rain today?
M : No, it was bright and sunny all morning. I can't believe this!
W : Me, either. The weather just changed in the blink of an eye.
M : Must be global warming.
W : Well, I don't know about that.

W：今日は雨になるって知ってた？
M：ううん。午前中ずっと明るくて晴れていたじゃない。こんな風になるなんて信じられない！
W：私も。天気が一瞬にして変わったもんね。
M：地球温暖化のせいに違いないよ。
W：うーん、それはどうかなぁ。

② have a grip on ～：～を把握する
have got it all figured out：全て把握している、何をどうすべきかすべてわかっている

▶活用例
W : What's wrong? You look like you're in a world of mess.
M : Yeah, I am. I just really don't have a grip on things.
W : Really? But, you've always got it all figured out. What's up?
M : It's nothing specific. I just have more to do than I can handle.

W：どうしたの？　なんだか問題を抱え込んでいるみたいだけど。
M：うん、そうなんだ。ほんとに物事をしっかり把握してないんだよね。
W：ほんとに？　でも、あなたはどんなことでも、いつもきちんとわかっていたじゃない。何があったの？
M：特にこれっていうのがあるわけじゃないんだけど。やらなくちゃならないことが、手に負えないぐらいたくさんあってね。

*S look like S V.：S は V するようだ
*be in a world of mess：大きな問題を抱えている

③ slip by ～：～の頭から抜け落ちる

▶活用例
M : I think you forgot to put a stamp on this envelope.
W : Really? I thought I got all of them.
M : Well, apparently not this one.
W : I guess it slipped by me. Here, I'll take care of it.

M：この封筒に切手を貼るのを忘れてたみたいだよ。
W：ほんとに？　全部に貼ったと思っていたけど。
M：うーん、どうもこれには貼ってないよ。

SONG #4 Nothing You Can Do

W：抜けちゃったみたいね。はい、やっておくわ。

*forget to ー：ーするのを忘れる

④ haven't got a clue：わからない

▶活用例
W : Have you seen Sean?
M : No, not since lunch.
W : Do you know where I could find him?
M : Sorry, I really haven't got a clue.

W：ショーン見かけた？
M：ううん、昼食の後は見てないけど。
W：どこに行けば見つかるかわかる？
M：ごめん、全然わかんないや。

⑤ any way you look at it：どう見ても

▶活用例
M : I'm thinking about buying some stocks.
W : Really? It's dangerous you know. The stock market is crazy!
M : Yeah, but if you do some research, you can find some pretty safe stocks. Also, my friend made a lot of money. And also…
W : You know. Any way you look at it, it's still really risky.

M：株を買おうかと思っているんだけど。
W：ほんと？　危ないんじゃない。株式相場って、まともじゃないから！
M：うん、でもちょっと調べれば、結構安全な株も見つけられるよ。それに、僕の友達も大儲けしたんだ。それと・・・
W：あのね、どう見ても、それでもほんとに危険だわ。

⑥ be blocked at every turn：いたる所で行き詰っている

▶活用例
M : This is unbelievable!
W : What is?
M : I've been trying to schedule an appointment with the CEO of GDC, but no matter what I do, I'm blocked at every turn!
W : I know what you mean. It's nearly impossible to get a meeting with him.

M：信じられない！
W：何が？
M：GDCのCEOと会う約束を取り付けようとしてきたんだけど、何をやっても、いたる所で行き詰まりなんだ！
W：うん、わかるわ。彼とミーティングを持つのは不可能に近いわね。

*no matter what S V：何を**S**が**V**しても

⑦ be about to －：まさに－しようとしている

▶活用例
W : Jeff, I'd like you to make a few phone calls for me.
M : But, I'm about to leave. I have a meeting in half an hour.
W : Oh, OK. Then don't worry about it. I'll have Hugo take care of it.

W：ジェフ、私の代わりに何本か電話して欲しいんだけど。
M：でも、ちょうど出ようとしているところなんだ。30分後に会議があるから。
W：ああ、わかったわ。心配しないで。ヒューゴにやってもらうから。

*make a phone call：電話する
*have ～ －：～に－してもらう

⑧ crash and burn：おじゃんになる、大失敗に終わる

▶活用例
W : Are you ready for the show?
M : Not at all.
W : Oh, come on. You've been practicing for weeks.
M : Yeah, but I'm not ready. Oh, it's gonna crash and burn!

W：舞台に出る準備はできた？
M：全然だよ。
W：何言ってるのよぉ。何週間も練習してきたじゃない。
M：うん、でもまだだめなんだ。あー、きっと大失敗に終わるよ！

⑨ go smoothly：うまくいく

▶活用例
W : Oh! Hey, James! Long time no see!
M : Yeah. It's been a while.
W : So, how've you been?
M : Good. I've been good. Everything's going smoothly.

W：あら！　まあ、ジェームズ！　久しぶりね！
M：そうだね。久しぶりだよね。
W：で、元気だった？
M：うん。このところずっと調子いいんだ。全てがうまくいっている。

*Long time no see.：久しぶり
*How have you been?：元気でやってた？

▶SONG #4　Nothing You Can Do

⑩ turn ～ around：～をひっくり返す

▶活用例
M : Oh, this is terrible!
W : What's wrong?
M : Do you remember that meeting we had with Jared last week?
W : Sure, what about it?
M : Well, I forgot to send him an extra catalogue and now he says he wants to cancel his order.
W : Really? I'm sorry to hear that. A little mistake like that can turn it all around. I guess you've got to be more careful.

M：あー、ひどいなあ！
W：どうしたの？
M：先週のジャレドとの会議覚えている？
W：もちろん。それがどうしたの？
M：うん、彼に追加のカタログを送るのを忘れていたら、注文をキャンセルしたいって言うんだ。
W：ほんと？　お気の毒さま。そんなちょっとしたミスで全てがひっくり返っちゃうこともあるのね。もうちょっと気をつけなきゃいけないのかもね。

*What about it?：それがどうかしたの？

⑪ fall behind ～：～から遅れる

▶活用例
W : Hey, Jeff. You busy?
M : Yeah, actually, swamped. Why? What's up?
W : I was gonna ask if you could help me out a bit, but don't worry about it.
M : Yeah, sorry I can't. I'm falling behind everyone as it is.

W：ねぇ、ジェフ。忙しい？
M：うん、実際、滅茶苦茶忙しいんだ。なんで？　どうしたの？
W：ちょっと手伝ってもらえないか聞こうと思っていたんだけど、気にしないで。
M：うん、ごめん、できないや。もうすでに、皆から遅れちゃっているんだよね。

*as it is：もうすでに

⑫ be on the block：なくなる危機に瀕している

▶活用例
W : Jeff, you don't look so good. Something wrong?
M : Well, I've been making a lot of small, careless mistakes recently.
W : Has the boss said anything to you about it?
M : Yeah, basically that my job is on the block.

W：ジェフ、あまり元気がないみたいだけど。どうかしたの？

M：うん、最近、小さなケアレスミスをしてばっかりいるんだ。
W：そのことで、上司は何か言ってきた？
M：うん。簡単に言えば、僕が仕事を失いそうみたいなことをね。

⑬ **be on edge**：極限状態にいる、ピリピリしている、不安だ

▶活用例
W : You nervous about your date tonight?
M : Nervous? No! I'm totally, completely on edge!
W : Wow. You really should try and take it easy.

W：今夜のデートのことで不安になってるの？
M：不安？ それどころじゃないよ！ 完全に極限状態なんだ！
W：うわぁ。ほんと肩の力を抜くようにしたほうがいいわよ。

*__take it easy__：気楽にやる

⑭ **pull it off**：うまくやる

▶活用例
W : Did you hear that Ann closed a deal with GDC?
M : You're joking! I couldn't even get a meeting with them!
W : I know, but somehow she pulled it off.
M : Unbelievable.

W：アンがGDCとの商談をまとめたって聞いた？
M：冗談だろ！ 僕なんか、彼らとミーティングさえできなかったのに！
W：そうよね。でも彼女はどうにかしてうまくやったのよ。
M：信じられない。

*__close a deal with__ ~：~との商談をまとめる

⑮ **give it one's best**：全力を尽くしてやる

▶活用例
W : Excuse me, Sean?
M : Yes, boss?
W : I need someone to take over the GDC account. Think you can handle it?
M : Sure! I'll give it my best.

W：ちょっといいかしら、ショーン？
M：はい、社長、何か？
W：GDCとの取引を引き継ぐ人が必要なんだけど。どう、できる？
M：もちろんです！ 全力を尽くして頑張ります。

*__take over__：~を引き継ぐ

SONG #4 Nothing You Can Do

⑯ **cut ～ loose**：～を切り捨てる、～を解雇する
   let ～ go：、～を手放す、～を解雇する
   get laid off：リストラされる

▶活用例
W : I just heard that Jeff got laid off.
M : Really? They let him go?
W : Yeah. His performance was down, so I guess they had to cut him loose.
M : Wow. They're cutting back more than I thought.

W：ジェフがリストラされたって今聞いたんだけど。
M：ほんとに？　会社が彼を解雇しちゃったの？
W：うん。彼の成績が下がったから、解雇しなくちゃならなかったんだと思う。
M：わー。思っていた以上に会社は削減してるんだな。

＊**cut back**：削減する

⑰ **get to ～**：～を苦しめる、～に効く、～に到達する

▶活用例
W : Hey, you doing OK?
M : Actually, not really.
W : Your sales are still down, huh?
M : Yeah. I might even lose my job. It's really getting to me.

W：ねえ、大丈夫？
M：実は、そうでもないんだ。
W：あなたの売り上げが、まだ下がっているのね？
M：うん。仕事も失いかねない。ほんとにこたえてるよ。

⑱ **as if S V**：まるでSがVするかのように

▶活用例
M : Have you seen Adam today?
W : Yeah. He looks as if he didn't sleep at all last night.
M : Well, he probably didn't. He went out with Kyle.
W : Ah, that's why! Once Kyle starts drinking, he doesn't stop until at least 4:00 in the morning.

M：今日アダム見た？
W：ええ。昨夜、全然寝てないような様子よ。
M：うん、多分寝てないだろうね。彼はカイルと出かけたんだ。
W：ああ、それで！　カイルはいったん飲み始めると、少なくとも朝の4時までは飲み続けるものね。

⑲ **go from bad to worse**：ますます悪化する

▶活用例
M : Where's Chris?
W : Haven't you heard? He's really sick!
M : I thought he just had a cold.
W : He did, but it turned into pneumonia. Now he's in the hospital.
M : Really? It went from bad to worse, huh?

M：クリスはどこ？
W：聞いてないの？　彼、すごく具合が悪いのよ！
M：ただの風邪だと思っていたけど。
W：最初はね。でもそれが肺炎になっちゃったの。今、入院しているわ。
M：ほんと？　悪化しちゃったんだね。

***turn into** ～：～に変わる

⑳ **fall apart**：バラバラになる、崩壊する

▶活用例
W : Hey Jeff. You doing OK?
M : Actually, no, not really.
W : What's the matter?
M : Well, you know I got laid off, right? Also, my stocks all crashed. Amy and I had a big fight. It just seems like everything is falling apart.

W：ねえ、ジェフ。大丈夫？
M：実際、そうでもないなあ。
W：どうしたの？
M：うーん、君も知っている通り、僕は会社をリストラされたよね。その上、僕の持っている株がみんな暴落しちゃって。エイミーと僕は大喧嘩したんだ。全てが崩壊しつつある感じだよ。

* **～ ,right？**：～ですよね？
***It seems like S V.**：S は V するようだ

㉑ **go down the drain**：失敗に終わる

▶活用例
M : The boss just told me I've gotta scrap the current GDC project and start again from scratch.
W : What in the world for?
M : Well, he seemed fairly certain that if we went ahead as planned the whole project would end up going down the drain.
W : Really? Well, if he says so.

SONG #4　Nothing You Can Do

M：社長が今言ってきたんだけど、現在の GDC のプロジェクトを廃止して、もう一度最初からやり直さなきゃならないんだ。
W：一体全体どうして？
M：うーん、このプロジェクトを今の予定のままで進めると、プロジェクト全体が失敗に終わるって確信しているみたいだった。
W：ほんとに？　うーん、でも社長がそう言うんじゃねぇ。

*start from scratch：最初からやり直す
*in the world：一体全体
*go ahead：先に進む
*as planned：計画通りに

㉒ as for 〜：〜に関しては

▶活用例
M : What would you like us to do first?
W : Let's see. Tim, can you decorate the living room? And, Nick, why don't you clean the kitchen?
M : OK, and what are you going to do?
W : As for me, I'll have a beer and watch TV while you work.

M：僕達に最初に何をして欲しい？
W：えーと。ティム、居間の飾り付けをしてくれる？　そして、ニックはキッチンを片付けてくれない？
M：わかった。それで君は何をするの？
W：私は、二人が働いている間、ビールを飲みながらテレビでも見るわ。

㉓ see：交際する

▶活用例
M : Do you know if Amy's seeing anyone?
W : Yeah, actually she's going out with Jeff.
M : Jeff? Why? What does she see in him?
W : I don't know. Good question.

M：エイミーが誰かと付き合っているかどうか知っている？
W：うん、実はね、彼女はジェフと付き合っているの。
M：ジェフ？　なんで？　彼女は彼のどこがいいの？
W：わかんない。いい質問ね。

*go out with 〜：〜と交際する
*What do you see in 〜 ?：〜のどこがいいの？
*Good question.：いい質問だ（即答できない難題に対する返答を考える際に、時間稼ぎとして使うきまり表現）

SONG #5
Go On! Get Out!

▶ SONG #5
Go On! Get Out!

(Verse 1)
Forget it. I get it.
There's no need to explain.
Don't try it. I don't buy it.
You're lying to me again.

I knew it. Saw through it.
It's perfectly clear.
So let's just get it over with.
I just wanna be through with this.
I can't take any more of this.
I've had it up to here!

(Chorus)
Go on! Get out!
And don't ever come back.
I don't ever want to see you again.

I'm serious! I'm furious!
You pushed me till I snapped.
And now believe me when I say that it's the end.

(Verse 2)
That's it. It's over.
Just leave me alone.
I've had it. Can't stand it.
Now you're on your own.

I'm through with you.
There's nothing else to say.
So why don't we just call it quits?
Why don't we get on with it?
I can't handle any more of this.
Do me a favor and go away!

(Chorus)

(Bridge)
Get out of my face. Get off my case.
Don't think that I can't find someone to take your place.

You've broken my heart. You've torn me apart.
It's about time for you to be replaced.

(Chorus)

(Verse 3)
Come off it. Just drop it.
Don't say a thing.
Be quiet. Don't try it.
'Cause I'm not listening.

I mean it. Believe it.
I won't budge an inch.
There's nothing else that you can say.
There's no more games that you can play.
I don't understand you anyway.
You never ever make any sense!

(Verse 4)
How dare you? How could you?
It's hard to believe.
You used me, misused me.
And now you'd better leave.

Screw it. You blew it.
It's all your fault.
You thought you'd get away with it.
Didn't think you'd have to pay for it.
Maybe thought I'd be OK with it.
But you know what? I'm not!

(Chorus)

(Chorus)

(Verse 1)
もういいよ　わかってるから
説明なんていらない
そんなことしないで　もう信じないから
君はまた嘘をついている

分かってたんだ　全部お見通しさ
完璧に明らかだ
だからもう終わりにしよう
ただもう終わりにしたいんだ
もうこれ以上は無理
これ以上は我慢できない！

(Chorus)
早く行ってくれ！　出て行ってくれ！
もう二度と戻ってこないでほしい
君の顔なんて二度と見たくない

本気だよ！　怒り狂ってるんだ！
君は僕がキレるほど追い込んだ
嘘なんかじゃないよ　これが最後なんだ

(Verse 2)
もはやこれまで　もう終わり
放っておいてくれ
もう十分　これ以上は耐えられない。
君は一人ぼっち

君とはもう終わり
他に言うことはない
だから別れることにしよう
今すぐにでも
これ以上は僕の手に負えない
お願いだから　僕の前から消えてくれ！

(Chorus)

(Bridge)
僕の前から消えてくれ　もう干渉しないでほしい
君のかわりを見つけられないと思ったら大間違いさ

君は僕の心を傷つけた　僕を苦しめたんだ
そろそろ君には席を譲ってもらう時なのさ

(Chorus)

(Verse 3)
いい加減にしろよ　もうやめてくれ
何も言わないで
静かにして　試しても無駄さ
君の言うことなんか聞いていないから

本気だよ　信じてくれ
もう引き下がらない
君はもう何も言えない
君はゲーム・オーバー
どうせ君のことは理解できない
君の言っていることはいつも筋違いだ！

(Verse 4)
よくもそんなことを？　どうしたらそんなことを？
とても信じられない
君は僕を利用した　悪用したんだよ
だから君はもう去ったほうがいい

もういいよ　君はしくじったんだ
全部君のせいさ
君はうまくやりおおせると思っていたんだろう
報いを受ける必要なんかないと思ってたのさ
僕なら大丈夫だろうとでも思ってたのかもしれない
でもね…　僕は大丈夫なんかじゃないんだよ！

(Chorus)

(Chorus)

▶SONG #5　Go On! Get Out!

曲解説

　4曲目では、あまりの状況の急変に呆然自失の主人公でしたが、ふと我に帰ると彼女に対する怒りが沸々と湧き上がってきます。この曲では、主人公は自らを省みることなく、全てを彼女のせいにして、ありとあらゆる罵詈雑言を彼女に向かって投げつけています。

　まず彼は彼女を嘘つきと決め付けます（**Forget it. I get it. There's no need to explain. Don't try it. I don't buy it. You're lying to me again.**）。そして、キレる程に自分を追い込んだのは彼女のほうだと言い放ちます（**You've pushed me till I snapped.**）。

　その後は、ありとあらゆる言葉を使って別れを迫ります（**That's it. It's over. I'm through with you. So why don't we just call it quits. Why don't we get on with it? It's about time for you to be replaced.**）。

　歌詞のほとんどは、彼女に対する激しい言葉で埋め尽くされていますが、実は、8曲目で明らかになる、このアルバムにおける最大のテーマにつながる大事な文が2つ、さりげなく出てきます。それは、**I don't understand you anyway. You never ever make any sense!** という2文です。この2文がどういう意味を持つのか考えつつ、8曲目を楽しみにして聴き続けていただければと思います。

　この曲では様々な効果音を聞くことができます。それらはフライパンや魔法瓶等、台所にある様々なものを駆使し、それらから生じる音をデジタル処理して作ったものです。

I．学習用歌詞

(Verse 1)
Forget it.
1
I **get it**.
 2
There's no need to explain.
Don't try it.
I **don't buy it**.
 3
You're lying to me again.
    A

I knew it.
Saw through it.
3
It's perfectly clear.
So let's just **get it over with**.
               4
I just wanna **be through with** this.
              5
I **can't take any more of** this.
  6
I**'ve had it up to here**!
 7

(Chorus)
Go on!
8
Get out!
8
And don't ever come back.
         B
I don't ever want to see you again.

I'm serious!
I'm furious!
You've pushed me till I **snapped**.
              C   9
And now believe me when I say that it's the end.

(Verse 2)
That's it.
10

SONG #5 — Go On! Get Out!

It's over.
Just **leave** me **alone**.
　　　11
I've had it.
Can't stand it.
Now you're **on your own**.
　　　　　12

I'm through with you.
　5
There's nothing else to say.
So why don't we just **call it quits**?
　　　　　　　　　　　3
Why don't we **get on with it**?
　　　　　　　13
I can't **handle** any more of this.
　　　14
Do me a favor and go away!
15

(Chorus)

(Bridge)
Get out of my face.
16
Get off my case.
17
Don't think that I can't find someone to **take your place**.
　D　　　　　　　　　　　　　　　　18

You've broken my heart.
You've **torn** me **apart**.
　　　19
It's about time for you **to** be replaced.
20

(Chorus)

(Verse 3)
Come off it.
21
Just **drop it**.
　9

Don't say a thing.
Be quiet.
Don't try it.
'Cause I'm not listening.

I mean it.
Believe it.
I won't **budge an inch**.
    22

There's nothing else that you can say.
There's no more games that you can play.
I don't understand you anyway.
You never ever **make** any **sense**!
         2

(Verse 4)
How dare you?
E

How could you?
It's hard to believe.
You used me, misused me.
And now you'd better leave.

Screw it.
23
You **blew it**.
   24
It's all your fault.
You thought you'd **get away with it**.
         25
Didn't think you'd have to **pay for** it.
         26
Maybe thought I'd be OK with it.
But **you know what**?
   27
I'm not!

(Chorus)

(Chorus)

▶SONG #5　Go On! Get Out!

II. 語句解説

A. lying
　この lying の原形は lie で「嘘をつく」という意味です。この lie の場合は lie-lied-lied-lying と変化します。
　lie には「横になる」という意味の lie もあり、この lie と「横たえる」という意味の lay の活用は混同しやすいので、しっかり覚えておく必要があります。lie は lie-lay-lain-lying と変化し、lay は lay-laid-laid-laying と変化します。

B. ever
　この ever や歌詞の中の次の行に出てくる ever のように、禁止の命令文や否定文の中に出てくる ever は「絶対に」とか「二度と」という意味になって、否定の意味合いを強調します。

C. till
　till と by はよく混同されますが、till は「～まで」と動作・状態の継続の終了時を表わす一方、by は「～までに」と動作の完了の最終期限を表わします。
　また、till には前置詞と接続詞の両方の用法があるのに対して、by には接続詞としての用法はありません。

D. Don't think
　この Don't think は主語が省略されているのではなく、禁止の命令文で、「考えるな」という意味になっています。

E. How dare you?
　ここでは、意味上は you の後ろに break my heart、tear me apart といった語句が省略されていると考えることもできますが、How dare you? だけで、「よくもそんなことを」とか「よくもまあ」といった意味で用いられます。

III. 重要表現

① Forget it.：もういいよ

▶活用例
W : Hey Simon, can you do me a favor?
M : Hold on a sec.
W : It won't take long, just…
M : Just give me a minute, OK?
W : Forget it. I'll take care of it myself.

W：ねえ、サイモン、ちょっとお願いがあるんだけど？
M：ちょっと待って。
W：時間はかからないから。ちょっと…
M：少しだけ待って、いい？
W：もういいわ。自分でやるから。

*Can you do me a favor?：お願いがあるんだけど
*Hold on a sec.：ちょっと待って
*take care of 〜：〜を処理する

② get it：理解する
make sense：意味をなす、道理にかなう

▶活用例
W : OK, did that make sense?
M : Yes, I got it. It's perfectly clear except for that last part.
W : OK. I'll go over it one more time.

W：さてと、意味わかった？
M：うん、わかった。明確になったよ。最後のところ以外はね。
W：じゃあ、もう一度説明するわね。

*except for 〜：〜を除いて
*go over 〜：〜を説明する

③ don't buy it：信じない
see through 〜：〜の正体を見抜く
call it quits：終わりにする

▶活用例
M : She told him she was out with Mari but…
W : But what? He didn't buy it?
M : Nope. He saw right through it, even called Mari to check.
W : Ooh, I guess they're gonna call it quits then, huh?

M：彼女は彼に、マリと出かけたって言ったんだけど・・・
W：だけど何？　彼は信じなかったの？
M：そう。彼は簡単に見抜いて、マリに電話してチェックまでしたんだ。
W：わー、じゃあ、彼らは別れるのかしら？

SONG #5 Go On! Get Out!

④ get it over with：けりをつける、終わりにする

▶活用例
M : I really hate writing these weekly reports.
W : Yeah, me, too.
M : I guess there's no way around it though, huh?
W : That's true. Well, we might as well get it over with.

M：ほんとにこの週報を書くの嫌いなんだよね。
W：うん、私も。
M：でも避けて通れないしなー。
W：ほんとね。まぁ、私達もさっさと片付けちゃったほうがいいわね。

*way around 〜：〜を回避する方法
*might as well ー：ーしたほうがいい

⑤ be through with 〜：〜を終えている

▶活用例
W : I can't wait to finish this project!
M : Me, too. We should be done in about two weeks, right?
W : Yeah, I think so. And then, when we are through with it, we'll finally get a vacation.
M : Yeah, that will be so nice!

W：このプロジェクトが終わるのが待ちきれないわ！
M：僕もだよ。だいたい２週間後には終わっているはずだよね？
W：うん、そう思うわ。そして、これが終わればついに休暇よ。
M：うん、最高だろうね！

*be done：終わった、完了した

⑥ can't take any more of 〜：〜にはもう我慢の限界だ

▶活用例
M : I'm really gonna go crazy.
W : Why? What's wrong?
M : My girlfriend and I just keep fighting and fighting all the time.
W : That's no fun.
M : Yeah, I really can't take any more of this.

M：ほんとに頭がおかしくなりそうだ。
W：なんで？　何があったの？
M：彼女といつも喧嘩ばかりしててさぁ。
W：それじゃあ楽しくないわね。
M：うん、もうほんとに我慢の限界だよ。

*go crazy：気が狂う
*all the time：いつも

⑦ have had it up to here：これ以上我慢できない

▶活用例
W : Look, maybe we should break up.
M : How dare you say that?
W : Oh, come on! We've both had it up to here!
M : Yeah, but I think we can work it out.

W：ねぇ、聞いて。多分私達は別れたほうがいいのかも。
M：よくもそんなことが言えるね。
W：ねぇ、いい加減にしてよ！　私達二人とも、もう限界まで来てるでしょ！
M：うん、でも僕は、なんとか上手く解決できると思っているんだ。

*break up：別れる
*How dare S − ?：よくも S は−できるものだ
*work ～ out：～をなんとか解決する

⑧ Go on!：出て行け！
　Get out!：消えうせろ！

▶活用例
W : How could you do this to me?!
M : What are you talking about? You're acting crazy!
W : No, I am not! You lied again! Admit it!
M : I did not! You're out of your mind!
W : That's it! Get out! Go on, and don't come back!
M : Fine! I won't! Bye.

W：よくもこんなことが私にできたわねぇ？！
M：なんのこと？　頭がおかしくなったみたいだよ！
W：おかしくなんかないわ！　またあなた嘘をついたでしょ！　認めなさいよ！
M：ついてないよ！　気でも狂ったんじゃない！
W：もう十分！　出て行って！　早く行って、もう戻ってこないで！
M：わかったよ！　帰ってくるもんか！　バイバイ。

*How could S − ?：よくも S は−できたものだ
*be out of one's mind：気が狂っている

SONG #5　Go On! Get Out!

⑨ **snap**：感情をぶちまける、キレる
drop it：（議論などを）やめる

▶活用例

W : I'm sorry I snapped at you yesterday.
M : It's OK. It was my fault. I made you so angry.
W : No, it wasn't your fault. I shouldn't have snapped.
M : Well, OK. Let's just drop it.

W：昨日は感情的になっちゃってゴメンね。
M：いいよ。僕のせいなんだ。僕が君を怒らせちゃったんだよ。
W：ううん、あなたのせいなんかじゃないわよ。あなたに食って掛かったりするべきじゃなかったわ。
M：まぁ、いいじゃない。その話はもうやめようよ。

*shouldn't have p.p.：～すべきではなかったのに（してしまった）

⑩ **That's it.**：それで終わりだ、ただそれだけ

▶活用例

W : Is Andy back from lunch yet?
M : No, not yet. He's been gone for almost two hours.
W : Again? That's it. I'm going to go talk to the boss about this.

W：アンディーはもう昼食から帰ってきた？
M：いや、まだだよ。もう2時間くらいになるね。
W：また？　もういいわ。上司にこのことを言いに行く。

*go talk to ～：～に話しに行く

⑪ **leave ～ alone**：～をそっとしておく

▶活用例

M : I've got a couple questions.
W : Um, can they wait? I'm really busy right now.
M : Yeah, but I just want to know…
W : Did you hear what I said? I'm really busy!
M : Yeah, I heard you, but…
W : Listen! Ask somebody else! Please, leave me alone!

M：2、3質問があるんだけど。
W：うーん、ちょっと待ってくれない？　今、ほんとに忙しいのよ。
M：うん、でもちょっと知りたくて・・・
W：私の言ったこと、聞こえなかった？　ほんとに忙しいの！
M：うん、聞こえたよ。でも・・・
W：ちょっと！　誰か別の人に聞いてよ！　お願いだから放っておいて！

⑫ on one's own：一人で、自力で

▶活用例
M : I'm thinking of quitting.
W : What? Are you serious? Why?
M : Well, I've been working here for a long time, and I'm thinking of starting my own company.
W : Really? You think you can make it on your own?
M : I'm not sure, but I want to try.

M：辞めようかなって思っているんだ。
W：何ですって？　本気なの？　どうして？
M：うん、ここも長いし、自分の会社を興そうかと思っているんだ。
W：ほんと？　自力でやっていける目途がついているのね。
M：確信はないけど、トライしてみたいんだよ。

⑬ get on with it：やるべきこと急いでをやり始める

▶活用例
M : I'm really not in the mood to clean right now.
W : Me, either. But we gotta do it.
M : Yeah, I know.
W : Come on. Let's get on with it. It won't take too long.

M：今は掃除する気分じゃないなあ。
W：私も。でもやらなくちゃ。
M：うん、わかってる。
W：さあ、さっさと始めましょう。そんなにかからないわよ。

*be in the mood to －：－する気になっている

⑭ handle：対処する、行う、耐える

▶活用例
W : Hey Jeff, when was the last time you had a good night's sleep?
M : Why? Do I look tired or something?
W : Well, yeah, actually. You do.
M : Honestly, I've been so busy. I really don't know how much longer I can handle it.

W：ねえ、ジェフ。いつからぐっすり眠れてないの？
M：なんで？　疲れているように見える？
W：うーん、まぁ、ほんとのこと言って、そう見えるわ。
M：実際、このところすごく忙しくて。この先どのくらいこんな状況に対処していけるかわからないよ。

SONG #5 Go On! Get Out!

⑮ Do me a favor and − .：お願いだから−してください

▶活用例
W : Are you busy right now?
M : Not really. What's up?
W : Do me a favor and copy this report for me.
M : OK. Just a second.

W：今忙しい？
M：そうでもないけど。どうしたの？
W：お願いなんだけど、このレポートをコピーしてくれない？
M：いいよ。ちょっと待ってね。

⑯ get out of one's face：～の前から去る

▶活用例
W : You OK, Jeff?
M : Kind of. The boss has been on my case all week.
W : Yeah, I know. He's stressed out about the convention.
M : Well, so am I, but I wish he would get out of my face.

W：ジェフ、大丈夫？
M：まーね。今週中ずっと上司が僕にうるさく言ってきて。
W：うん、知ってる。彼はコンベンションのことでイライラしてるのよ。
M：えー、僕だってそうだよ。でもほんとに僕の目の前から消え失せてくれればいいのに。

*be on one's case：～にうるさくしてくる
*be stressed out：イライラしている

⑰ get off one's case：～にうるさく言わない、～をそっとしておく

▶活用例
W : Why didn't you do the laundry?
M : I was too busy cleaning everything else!
W : Well, what about the kitchen? It looks horrible!
M : I cleaned all afternoon! I'm sorry if it's not perfect! Please, just get off my case!

W：なんで洗濯しなかったの？
M：それ以外の全てをきれいにするのに忙しかったんだよ！
W：じゃあ、キッチンはどうなの？　かなりひどいけど！
M：午後中片付けたんだよ！　完璧じゃなくて悪かったね！　お願いだから干渉しないでくれる！

*do the laundry：洗濯する
*be busy − ing：−するのに忙しい

⑱ take one's place：〜の代わりをする、〜の後任になる

▶活用例
W : Are you free on Saturday afternoon?
M : Yeah, why?
W : I was planning to play mahjong, but I have to go out of town on business. Can you take my place?
M : Sure! It's no problem.

W：土曜日の午後、暇？
M：うん。なんで？
W：マージャンをする予定だったんだけど、出張しなくちゃならないの。かわりにやってくれない？
M：もちろん！ 全然構わないよ。

*__no problem__：構わない、大丈夫

⑲ tear 〜 apart：〜の心を引き裂く、〜を苦しめる、〜をけなす

▶活用例
W : I really can't stand this anymore.
M : What's wrong?
W : Oh, we had another fight last night.
M : I'm sorry to hear that.
W : Yeah, it's been happening so often recently. It's really tearing me apart.

W：ほんとにこれ以上我慢できない。
M：どうしたの？
W：うん、昨夜また喧嘩したのよ。
M：お気の毒に。
W：ええ、最近しょっちゅうなの。ほんとに辛いわ。

*__be sorry to hear 〜__：〜を聞いて気の毒に思う

⑳ It's about time for 〜 to －．：そろそろ〜が－してもいい頃だ、そろそろ〜が－する時間だ

▶活用例
M : Do you know what time it is?
W : Yeah, it's 11:30.
M : Already? Well, I guess it's about time for me to go. My last train is coming soon.

M：何時だかわかる？
W：うん、11時半よ。
M：もう？ じゃあ、そろそろ行く時間かな。終電がもうすぐ来るんだ。

▶SONG #5　Go On! Get Out!

㉑ Come off it.：馬鹿なことを言うな、嘘をつくな

▶活用例
W : Where were you last night?
M : I was out with Sean and James.
W : Please don't lie to me.
M : Really! We went to…
W : Oh, come off it! I talked to Sean. He said you weren't with him last night.
M : Oh.

W：昨日の夜、どこに行ってたの？
M：ショーンとジェームズと出かけていたよ。
W：嘘つかないで。
M：ほんとだよ！　僕たちは一緒に出かけて……
W：いい加減にしてよ！　ショーンともう話ししたんだから。昨晩あなたとは一緒じゃなかったって言ってたわ！
M：あー。

㉒ budge an inch：譲る

▶活用例
W : I think we should reschedule the meeting.
M : I do, too, but the boss won't let us.
W : What if I try to talk to him?
M : It's no use. He won't budge an inch.

W：ミーティングの予定を変更するべきだと思うんだけど。
M：僕もそう思う。でも上司がそうさせてはくれないよ。
W：私が彼と話してみたらどうなるだろう？
M：無駄だよ。彼は頑として引かないよ。

*What if S V ?：もし S が V したとしたらどうなるだろう？
*no use：無駄な

㉓ Screw it.：【卑】もう駄目だ、もういいよ

▶活用例
W : You really should tell her the truth.
M : Yeah, I know, but it's really hard.
W : Of course it is, but it's the only choice you've got.
M : Screw it. You're right. I'll talk to her tonight.

W：彼女に本当のことを言うべきよ。
M：うん、わかっている、でもほんとにつらいんだよ。
W：そりゃそうよ。でもそれしかあなたに選ぶ道はないわ。
M：もう駄目だ。君の言う通り。今夜彼女に話すよ。

㉔ blow it：台無しにする、しくじる

▶活用例
W : So, how did the presentation go?
M : I completely blew it.
W : Oh no! What happened?
M : Well, first my computer froze, then I froze, and well, you get the picture.

W：それで、プレゼンはどうだった？
M：完璧にしくじっちゃったよ。
W：え、うそ！　何があったの？
M：うーんと、まず僕のコンピューターがフリーズして、僕もかたまっちゃって、それで、まぁわかるでしょ？

*freeze：(コンピューターが) フリーズする
*get the picture：状況を理解する

㉕ get away with it：罰せられずにやりおおせる、処罰をのがれる

▶活用例
W : Did you hear that the mayor is going to jail?
M : No, I didn't! Is it because of the bribes?
W : Yep. He thought he could get away with it, but somebody told the police.

W：市長が収監されるって聞いた？
M：いや、聞いてないよ！　例の賄賂の件で？
W：そう。市長はうまくのがれることができるって思ったんでしょうけど、誰かが警察に垂れ込んだのよ。

*go to jail：収監される
*because of 〜：〜のせいで

㉖ pay for 〜：〜の償いをする、〜の報いを受ける

▶活用例
M : So, how long is the mayor going to be in prison?
W : The judge sentenced him to three years.
M : Three years? Wow! That's a long time!
W : Yeah, but he accepted a lot of bribes. Now he's gotta pay for it.

M：それで、市長はどのくらい収監されるの？
W：裁判官は、懲役３年の判決を言い渡したの。
M：３年？　わー！　それは長いね！
W：ええ。でも彼は賄賂をたくさん受け取ったから。罪を償わないと。

*sentence 〜 to …years：〜に懲役…年の判決を言い渡す

SONG #5 Go On! Get Out!

㉗ You know what?：あのね、いいかい

▶活用例
M : I'm having trouble finding a restaurant for our end of the year party.
W : How many places have you called?
M : Ten! Everything is booked!
W : You know what? Let's just have the party here in the office. We'll order pizza.

M：僕達の忘年会をやるレストランを見つけるのに苦労しているんだ。
W：いくつのレストランに電話したの？
M：10！どこも予約で一杯なんだ！
W：ねえ、会社でやりましょうよ。ピザを注文して。

*have trouble － ing：－するのに苦労する

▶ **SONG #6**
I'm Sorry

SONG #6

I'm Sorry

(Verse 1)
I never meant to hurt you.
I never meant to say what I said.
I went way overboard.
I was way out of my head.

I never meant to doubt you.
Never meant to lose control.
Somehow I got way out of line.
Now I may have to let you go.

(Pre-Chorus)
I wish I hadn't been so mean.
I wish I had a time machine.
Right now, I'd do anything,
For you to be back here with me.
But all I can do is say.

(Chorus)
I'm sorry. I'm so sorry.
I wish that there were something I could do.
I'm sorry. I'm so sorry
I wish that I could make it up to you.
I'm sorry. I'm sorry. I'm sorry.
I'm so sorry. So sorry. So sorry.

(Verse 2)
I know that I blew my stack.
And I'm sorry that I snapped.
If you hadn't pushed my buttons,
I never would've cracked.

I'm not saying that it's your fault.
I'm not saying that you're to blame.
I was the one who flipped out.
I was the one acting insane.

(Pre-Chorus)

(Chorus-Different Lyrics)
I'm sorry. I'm so sorry.
I wish that there were something I could do.
I'm sorry. I'm so sorry
I wish that I could make it up to you.
I'm sorry. I'm sorry. I'm so sorry.
I'm sorry. I'm sorry. So sorry.

(Verse 3)
I feel so stupid.
I feel like such a jerk.
I wanna patch things up.
I want to make this work.

I don't know if you can forgive me.
I don't know if you can wait.
I'm scared of hearing you say,
"I'm afraid it's too late."

(Pre-Chorus-Different Lyrics)
I wish I had a time machine.
I wish I hadn't been so mean.
Right now, I'd do anything,
For you to be back here with me.
But all I can do is say.

(Chorus-Different Lyrics)
I'm sorry. I'm so sorry.
Somehow I will make it up to you.
I'm sorry. I'm so sorry
There's something I want to say to you.
I miss you. I miss you. I miss you.
I miss you. I miss you. I miss you.

(Verse 1)
傷つけるつもりなんてまったくなかった
あんなふうに言うつもりはなかった
言い過ぎてしまったんだ
頭がおかしくなってしまっていたんだ

本気で君を疑うつもりなんてなかった
本気でキレるつもりはなかった
でもなぜか言い過ぎてしまったんだ
そして今　僕は君を手放さなくてはならないか
もしれない

(Pre-Chorus)
あんなに意地悪くしなければよかった
タイムマシーンがあればいいのに
今なら　僕はなんでもするよ
君が僕の元へ戻ってきてくれるためならば
でも今できることは　ただこう言うことだけ

(Chorus)
ごめん　本当にごめん
何か僕にできることがあればいいのに
ごめん　本当にごめん
償いができたらいいのに
ごめん　ごめん　ごめん
本当に本当にごめんなさい　許してほしい

(Verse 2)
キレちゃったんだよ
そんなことをしてごめん
もし君が僕を怒らせるようなことをしなければ
理性を失ったりはしなかったのに

でも君のせいだなんて言ってるわけじゃない
君を責めているわけじゃない
カッとなったのは僕
僕が正気を失っていただけなんだ

(Pre-Chorus)

(Chorus-Different Lyrics)
ごめん　本当にごめん
何か僕にできることがあればいいのに
ごめん　本当にごめん
君に償いができたらいいのに
ごめん　ごめん　本当にごめん

ごめんなさい　本当に

(Verse 3)
本当に僕はバカだ
全くひどい奴だよ
元に戻りたい
上手くいったらいいのに

君が僕を許してくれるかどうかわからない
君が待ってくれるかどうかわからない
君がこう言うのを聞くのが怖い
「もう手遅れだと思うわ」

(Pre-Chorus-Different Lyrics)
タイムマシーンがあればいいのに
君にあんなにつらく当たらなければよかった
今なら　僕は何でもするよ
君が戻ってきてくれるためならば
でも今できることは　ただこう言うことだけ

(Chorus-Different Lyrics)
ごめん　本当にごめん
何とか君に償うよ
ごめん　本当にごめん
君に伝えたいことがある
君がいなくて寂しい　寂しい　寂しいんだ
君がいなくて寂しい　寂しいんだ　君がいなく
て……

▶ SONG #6　I'm Sorry

曲解説

　5曲目では激しく彼女を詰り、別れを切り出した主人公ですが、冷静になってみると自分も悪かったということに気付きます。

　この曲ではボサノバ風のリズムに乗った悲しげなメロディーの中で、主人公の後悔に満ちた心情が切々と歌い上げられています。

　まず主人公は、彼女に対して激しい言葉を浴びせたことに関して、自分がどうかしてたと言い (**I went way overboard. I was way out of my head.**)、それを後悔すると共に、時間が元に戻ればと願います (**I wish I hadn't been so mean. I wish I had a time machine.**)。

　そして、彼女が自分のところに戻ってきてくれるためなら何でもすると言いながらも (**Right now, I'd do anything for you to be back here with me.**)、現実的に自分にできることは謝ることだけだ (**But all I can do is say. I'm sorry. I'm so sorry.**) という弱気な状態に陥ります。

　主人公の心を支配しているのは、彼女を失うことに対する恐れと (**I'm scared of hearing you say, "I'm afraid it's too late."**)、彼女に償いたいという気持ち (**Somehow I will make it up to you.**)、そして何より、彼女がいなくて寂しい (**I miss you.**) という切実な思いなのです。

　この曲では、くどいほど **I'm sorry.** というフレーズが繰り返されます。喧嘩をした後、自分の方から悪かったと謝るのは難しいものです。しかし、この言葉こそが二人の関係を修復へと向かわせる魔法の言葉となります。自分の気持ちをしっかり言葉に表すことの重要性が、このアルバムの大きなテーマの一つです。

I. 学習用歌詞

(Verse 1)
I never **meant to** hurt you.
　　　　1
I never meant to say what I said.
I **went** way **overboard**.
　2　　　A
I **was** way **out of my head**.
　3

I never meant to doubt you.
Never meant to **lose control**.
　　　　　　　　　4
Somehow I **got** way **out of line**.
　　　　　5
Now I may have to let you go.

(Pre-Chorus)
I wish I hadn't been so mean.
B

I wish I had a time machine.
C
Right now, I'd do anything for you to be back here with me.
　　　　　　　　　　　　　　　　D
But **all** I **can do is** say.
　　　6

(Chorus)
I'm sorry.
I'm so sorry.
I wish that there were something I could do.
I'm sorry.
I'm so sorry.
I wish that I could **make it up** to you.
　　　　　　　　　7
I'm sorry.
I'm sorry.
I'm sorry.
I'm so sorry.
So sorry.
So sorry.

▶ SONG #6   I'm Sorry

(Verse 2)
I know that I **blew my stack**.
            8
And I'm sorry that I snapped.

If you hadn't **pushed my buttons**, I never would've cracked.
E   9

I'm not saying that **it's your fault**.
            10
I'm not saying that you**'re to blame**.
            10
I was the one who **flipped out**.
            10
I was the one acting insane.
      F

(Pre-Chorus)

(Chorus)
I'm sorry.
I'm so sorry.
I wish that there were something I could do.
I'm sorry.
I'm so sorry.
I wish that I could make it up to you.
I'm sorry.
I'm sorry.
I'm so sorry.
I'm sorry.
I'm sorry.
So sorry.

(Verse 3)
I feel so stupid.
I feel like such a **jerk**.
          11
I wanna **patch things up**.
    12
I want to **make** this **work**.
      13

I don't know **if** you can forgive me.
                14
I don't know if you can wait.
I'm scared of hearing you say, "**I'm afraid** it's too late."
 15   16

(Pre-Chorus-Different Lyrics)
I wish I had a time machine.
I wish I hadn't been so mean.
Right now, I'd do anything for you to be back here with me.
But all I can do is say.

(Chorus-Different Lyrics)
I'm sorry.
I'm so sorry.
Somehow I will make it up to you.
I'm sorry.
I'm so sorry
There's something I want to say to you.
I miss you.
I miss you.
I miss you.
I miss you.
I miss you.
I miss you.

▶ SONG #6　I'm Sorry

II. 語句解説

A. way
　この way は副詞で、「はるかに」とか「ずっと」という意味です。

B. I wish I hadn't been so mean.
〈I wish I had p.p.〉で、「−したらよかったのに」という意味になり、過去の事実とは反する願望を表現する時に用います。この文の場合は、「実際には自分はとても意地悪だったんだけど、あんなに意地悪じゃなかったらよかったのに」という願望を表わしています。

C. I wish I had a time machine.
〈I wish I 過去形.〉で、「−すればいいのに」という意味になり、現在の事実とは反する願望を表現する時に用います。この文の場合は、「実際にはタイムマシーンを持っていないんだけれど、タイムマシーンを持っていればいいのに」という願望を表わしています。

D. I'd do anything for you to be back here with me
I'd は I would を短縮したものであり、この文は仮定法の文になっています。この文においては、if 節の代わりに for 以下が仮定条件を表わしています。つまり、「君が僕の元に戻ってくるためだったら、僕はどんなことでもするのに」ということです。

E. If you hadn't pushed my buttons, I never would've cracked.
〈If S1 had p.p., S2 would have p.p.〉というのは仮定法過去完了という形で、過去の事実に反する仮定や想像を表現する形です。「もし S1 が…したとしたら、S2 は−しただろうに」という意味になります。この文の場合は、「(実際には君は僕を怒らせるようなことをしたんだけど) もし僕を怒らせるようなことをしなかったら、(実際には僕はキレちゃったんだけど) 僕はキレなかっただろうに」という意味になります。

F. the one acting insane
　この acting は形容詞的用法の現在分詞で、「−している〜」という意味となって直前の one を修飾しています。ですから、この部分は、「正気ではない振舞いをしている人」という意味になります。

III. 重要表現

① mean to ～：～するつもりだ

▶活用例
W : Were you able to fix my air conditioner?
M : Well, I meant to fix it but actually, I think I made it worse.
W : What? Really?
M : Yeah, sorry. You should probably call a professional.

W：うちのエアコン、直せた？
M：うーん、直すつもりだったんだけど、実際のところ、悪化させちゃったみたい。
W：何ですって？　ほんと？
M：うん、ごめん。修理屋さんに電話したほうがいいと思うよ。

② go overboard：極端に走る、夢中にやる

▶活用例
W : What a great party! Who put this all together?
M : Oh, me and Ann, mostly. Mike helped a bit, too.
W : Well, it's fantastic. You guys really went overboard!
M : Well, we like to have a good time.

W：なんて素晴らしいパーティなんでしょう！　誰が企画したの？
M：ほとんど僕とアンだよ。マイクも少し手伝ってくれたけど。
W：うん、最高だわ。ほんとに夢中になって頑張っちゃったのね！
M：まぁ、楽しい時間を過ごしたいからね。

*put ～ together：～を企画する

③ be out of one's head：頭がどうかしている

▶活用例
W : Do you remember what you told me last night?
M : Um, not really. I was a little drunk.
W : You don't remember anything?
M : Well, some things. But I was pretty much out of my head.

W：昨夜私に言ったこと、覚えてる？
M：うーん、あまり覚えてないなあ。ちょっと酔っていたから。
W：何も覚えてないの？
M：まあ、少しは覚えているけど。でもかなりわけがわからなくなっていたんだ。

*not really：そうでもない
*pretty much：けっこう、ほとんど

▶ SONG #6　I'm Sorry

④ lose control：自制心を失う、カッとなる

▶活用例
W : I heard you went drinking with Simon last weekend.
M : Yep, but never again!
W : Why? What happened?
M : After one beer, he started yelling at people and making all kinds of trouble. He totally lost control!

W：先週末、サイモンと飲みに行ったって聞いたけど。
M：うん、でももう二度と行かない！
W：なんで？　どうしたの？
M：ビールを1杯飲んだら、サイモンが周りにいた人達に向かって怒鳴り始めて、ありとあらゆるトラブルを起こし始めたんだ。完全に理性を失っちゃったんだよ！

*go drinking with ～：～と飲みに行く
*yell at ～：～を怒鳴りつける

⑤ get out of line：間違ったことをやり過ぎる

▶活用例
M : Did he really do that?
W : Yeah, I couldn't believe it.
M : Wow, that's awful.
W : Yeah, no kidding. Sometimes he gets way out of line.

M：彼、ほんとにそんなことしたの？
W：うん、信じられなかったわ。
M：うわぁ、それはひどいね。
W：ほんと、冗談じゃないわ。彼は時々やり過ぎることがあるのよね。

*No kidding.：冗談じゃない、全くその通りだ

⑥ All S can do is ‒ .：Sにできるのは‒することだけだ

▶活用例
W : Did John send off all of his college applications?
M : Yeah, he sent the last one yesterday.
W : Do you think he'll get into the one he wants?
M : I don't know. All he can do now is wait.

W：ジョンは、大学の入学願書を全部発送したの？
M：うん、最後のを昨日送ってた。
W：希望の大学に入れると思う？
M：わからないなあ。彼に今できることは、待つことだけだね。

*send off ～：～を発送する
*get into ～：～に入学する

⑦ make it up to 〜：〜に償いをする

▶活用例
M : I'm so sorry about what I said.
W : It really hurt me, you know.
M : I know. I'm sorry. Let me make it up to you. Look, I really don't want to let you go.
W : Yeah, I know, but I need a little time.

M：この前言ったこと、ほんとにごめん。
W：すごく傷ついたのよ、わかるでしょ。
M：うん、ほんとにごめん。この償いはするから。ねぇ、ほんとに君を手放したりしたくないんだ。
W：うん、わかってる。でも少し時間がほしいの。

⑧ blow one's stack：キレる

▶活用例
M : I really didn't mean what I said. I was just upset.
W : Yeah, I know, but I'd never seen that side of you.
M : I usually have a lot of patience. I just couldn't control myself this time and I blew my stack.
W : Well, I kind of snapped, too.

M：僕の言ったことは本心じゃなかったんだ。ただイライラしてて。
W：うん、わかってるわ。でもあなたにあんな一面があるのを知らなかったから。
M：普通はもっと辛抱強いんだけど。ただ今回は自分で自分をコントロールできなくて、キレちゃったんだ。
W：まあ、私もちょっと感情的になっちゃったから。

⑨ push one's buttons：人の嫌がることをわざとする

▶活用例
W : So, why'd you get so angry?
M : Well, Amy knows what makes me upset and she just kept saying those things over and over again.
W : That's not very nice.
M : Well, we were fighting and she just kept pushing my buttons, and I finally cracked.

W：それで、なんでそんなに怒ったの？
M：だってエイミーは何ていったら僕が怒るかわかっていて、そういうことを何度も何度も言い続けたんだ。
W：それはよくないわね。
M：うん、僕達は喧嘩をしていて、彼女は僕の嫌がることをし続けた。それで僕はついにキレちゃったというわけ。

SONG #6　I'm Sorry

*over and over again：何度も何度も
*keep –ing：–し続ける

⑩ **It's one's fault.**：〜のせいだ
be to blame：責めを負うべきだ
flip out：カッとなる

▶活用例
M : I know it was all my fault. Can you forgive me?
W : Yeah, I guess so. I flipped out, too. So I'm also to blame.
M : Well, why don't we try to just let it go for now?
W : OK. Let's try to get back to normal.

M：全部僕のせいだってわかってるんだ。許してくれないかな？
W：うん、そうね。私もカッとなっちゃったから。私にも責任があるわ。
M：じゃあ、とりあえず、今回のことは忘れるように努力しようよ。
W：オッケー。元に戻るよう努力しましょう。

*let it go：それを忘れる
*get back to normal：元に戻る

⑪ **jerk**：馬鹿者、むかつく奴

▶活用例
M : So, do you think you can forgive him?
W : I don't know. He was being such a jerk!
M : Well, you two were having a fight. I'm sure you weren't being all that nice, either.
W : That's true. But still, I don't know.

M：そしたら、君は彼を許せそうなの？
W：わからない。あの時、彼はとっても嫌な奴だったのよ！
M：うーん、でも君達は喧嘩してたんでしょ。きっと君にも悪い所があったんだと思うけど。
W：それはそうね。でもまだ許せるかどうかわからないわ。

*have a fight：喧嘩する
*I'm sure S V.：きっと S は V する

⑫ patch things up：仲直りする

▶活用例
M：I really miss you.
W：Yeah, I miss you, too.
M：So, do you think we can get back together and patch things up?
W：I don't know. I'm still kind of upset.

M：君がいなくてほんとに寂しいんだ。
W：うん、私もよ。
M：じゃあ、僕たちもう一度元に戻ってやり直せるかな？
W：それはわからないわ。だって私はまだちょっと怒っているから。

*miss 〜：〜がいなくて寂しいと思う
*get back together：よりを戻す

⑬ make 〜 work：〜がうまく行くようにする

▶活用例
M：I'm sure we can fix this.
W：I don't know. We both have to change a lot.
M：Yeah, that's true. But, I think we can make this work.

M：きっと僕達は元に戻れるよ。
W：わからないわ。お互いにすごく変わらなくちゃね。
M：うん、それはその通りだ。でも僕達ならうまくやれると思うよ。

*fix：元の状態に戻す

⑭ if S V：S が V するかどうか

▶活用例
W：How was your job interview?
M：Terrible! It started off bad and then just got worse.
W：You know, if you hadn't worn that obnoxious tie, you probably would've made a better first impression.
M：That's true. I didn't care if they liked my tie. I was hoping they would like my personality.

W：就職の面接、どうだった？
M：ひどかったよ！　最初から嫌な感じで、どんどん悪い方に行っちゃった。
W：ねえ、もしあの感じの悪いネクタイをしていかなかったら、もっといい第一印象を与えられたんじゃない。
M：確かに。彼らが僕のネクタイを気に入るかどうかなんて、気にしてなかったんだ。僕の人柄を気に入ってくれると思っていたんだよ。

▶SONG #6　I'm Sorry

⑮ be scared of –ing：–するのが怖い

▶活用例
W : Have you tried calling Amy recently?
M : No, I'm too worried about what she'll say.
W : Really? Why?
M : I guess I'm just scared of making her more upset.

W：最近エイミーに電話してみた？
M：いや、彼女が何て言うかすごく心配で。
W：そうなの？　どうして？
M：彼女をもっと怒らせるのが怖いだけなんだと思うけど。

⑯ I'm afraid S V.：（残念ながら）S は V すると思う

▶活用例
W : Hello?
M : Hi, can I talk to Amy?
W : Oh, sorry. I'm afraid she's not in right now.
M : I see. Um, I'll try again later.

W：もしもし？
M：こんにちは。エイミーをお願いしたいんですが？
W：あぁ、ごめんなさい。彼女は今いません。
M：わかりました。えーっと、そしたらまた後でかけてみます。

*Can I talk to ～ ?：〈電話口で〉～さんいますか？
*be in：いる

▶ **SONG #7**
Take A Step Back

▶ SONG #7

Take A Step Back

(Verse1)
Sometimes, we find ourselves in a slump.
We don't know which way is up.
And we start thinking, "Maybe I should just give up."

Sometimes, it's totally out of our hands.
It doesn't go according to plan.
And these are the times when we have to do what we can.

At times, there's people who get in your way.
People who ruin your day.
And maybe you feel like you want to make them pay.

At times, you feel like you're on your own.
You feel like you're all alone.
And maybe you feel like you won't make it through the day.

(Chorus 1)
But take a step back,
And look at the big picture.
You'll see that it's really no big deal.
Of course you've had better days,
But you've also had worse.
Try not to lose track of what is real.

(Verse 2)
Sometimes, we don't see eye to eye.
No matter how hard we try,
We just end up making each other cry.

Sometimes, we try to get a point across.
But somehow the point gets lost.
And we don't know how or why.

At times, we tune each other out.
Other times we scream and shout.
And we don't even know what we're yelling about.

At times, we break each other's hearts.
We tear each other apart.
And we both just end up feeling down and out.

(Chorus 1)

(Chorus 2)
Take a step back,
And look at the big picture,
It's not the end of the world.
We will make it through,
All the ups and downs.
The trials of a boy and a girl.
The world of a boy and a girl.
The life of a boy and a girl.

(Verse1)
誰でも時にはスランプに陥ってしまう
困難な状況から抜け出す術もわからなくなり
「たぶんもう諦めるべきかもしれない」と思い始める

時々　まったく手に負えない事が起きる
物事は計画通りに進みやしない
そんな時には　できることをするだけ

時には　邪魔をする人が現れる
一日を台無しにしてしまう人が
そんなヤツらには償わせたいと感じるだろう

時には　自分は一人きりだと感じてしまう
一人っきりだという孤独感
そんな時は　一日ですら切り抜けることができない気になるかもしれない

(Chorus 1)
でも一歩下がって
全体を見てごらん
大したことないって気がつくから
もちろん　もっといい日もあっただろう
でももっと悪い日もあったはず
現実を見失わないようにすることが大切

(Verse 2)
時々　意見が合わないことがある
どんなに頑張ってみても
結局お互いを泣かせてしまう

大事なことを伝えようとしても
なぜだか伝わらないこともある
そして　その理由さえわからない

時々　僕達はお互いを無視してしまう
一方で　大声でわめき散らすこともある
何を叫んでいるかもわからないまま

時々　僕達はお互いを悲しませる
そしてお互いを苦しめる
結局はどちらも打ちのめされるだけ

(Chorus 1)

(Chorus 2)
一歩下がって
全体を見てごらん
この世の終わりってわけじゃないんだよ
僕達は切り抜けられるんだ
どんな浮き沈みでも
これが二人の試練
二人の世界
二人の人生

SONG #7　Take A Step Back

曲解説

　ピアノのアルペジオとジェフのギターに導かれて始まるこの曲は、悲しげな6曲目から一転して、とても穏やかで清らかな雰囲気を漂わせています。様々な妄想、狂気、ナイーブな幸福感とそれに続く喪失感。そして、抑えの利かない激情と後悔。そうした、人間の持つ手に負えない感情を経て辿り着いた悟りの境地。それがこの曲のテーマです。

　人はスランプに陥り、そこから抜け出す方法が分からない時があります（**Sometimes, we find ourselves in a slump. We don't know which way is up.**）。また、自分の邪魔をする人が現れたり（**At times, there's people who get in your way.**）、激しい孤独感に苛まれたりする時もあります（**At times, you feel like you're on your own.**）。こんな時は、一日たりとも切り抜けることはできないと感じてしまうものです（**And maybe you feel like you won't make it through the day.**）。

　しかし主人公はこう歌います。一歩下がって、全体を見てごらん。たいしたことないって気付くよ（**But take a step back and look at the big picture. You'll see that it's really no big deal.**）と。

　大事なことを伝えようにも伝わらないことがあります（**Sometimes, we try to get a point across. But somehow the point gets lost.**）。お互いを無視したかと思うと、大声でわめき散らしたりもします（**At times, we tune each other out. Other times we scream and shout.**）。そして、お互いを悲しませ（**At times, we break each other's hearts.**）、苦しめ（**We tear each other apart.**）、2人共打ちのめされてしまいます（**And we both just end up feeling down and out.**）。

　しかし、こんな時も、主人公は希望を捨てません。この世の終わりというわけではないからです（**It's not the end of the world.**）。

　あらゆる浮き沈みを切り抜けていくことが（**We will make it through all the ups and downs.**）、二人の試練であり、二人の世界であり、二人の人生なのです（**The trials of a boy and a girl. The world of a boy and a girl. The life of a boy and a girl.**）

I. 学習用歌詞

(Verse1)
Sometimes, we find ourselves **in a slump**.
　　　　　　　A　　　　　　　　1
We don't know **which way is up**.
　　　　　　　　　2
And we start thinking, "Maybe I should just give up."

Sometimes, it's totally **out of our hands**.
　　　　　　　　　　3
It doesn't **go according to plan**.
　　　　　　　4
And these are the times when we have to do what we can.
　　　　　　　B

At times, there's people who **get in your way**.
　　　　　　C　　　　　　　5
People who **ruin your day**.
D　　　　　6
And maybe you feel like you want to make them pay.

At times, you feel like you're on your own.
You feel like you're all alone.
　　　　　　　E
And maybe you feel like you won't **make it through** the day.
　　　　　　　　　　　　　　　7

(Chorus 1)
But take a step back and look at the **big picture**.
　　　　　　　　　　　　　　　8
You'll see that **it's** really **no big deal**.
　　　　　　　9
Of course you've had better days, but you've also had worse.
Try not to **lose track of** what is real.
F　　　　10　　　　　G

(Verse 2)
Sometimes, we don't **see eye to eye**.
　　　　　　　　　11
No matter how hard we try, we just **end up making** each other cry.
H　　　　　　　　　　　　　12

SONG #7   Take A Step Back

Sometimes, we try to **get** a point **across**.
               12
But somehow the point gets lost.
And we don't know how or why.

At times, we **tune** each other **out**.
           12
Other times we scream and shout.
And we don't even know what we're yelling about.

At times, we **break each other's hearts**.
           13
We tear each other apart.
And we both just end up feeling **down and out.**
                             14

(Chorus 1)

(Chorus 2)
Take a step back and look at the big picture.
It's not the end of the world.
14
We will **make it through** all the **ups and downs**.
        7   14
The trials of a boy and a girl.
I
The world of a boy and a girl.
J
The life of a boy and a girl.

II. 語句解説

A. find ourselves in a slump
この find は〈find O C〉という第5文型を作っており、「O が C という状態にいることに気付く」という意味です。ここでは O が ourselves、C が in a slump で、「自分自身がスランプに陥っているということに気付く」という意味になっています。

B. the times when we have to do what we can
when は関係副詞で、when 以下が times を修飾しています。「時」、どういう時かというと、「私達ができることをしなければならない」時ということです。

C. there's people
there's は there is の短縮形です。主語は people ということで複数なので、be 動詞はそれに対応して are となるべきですが、実際には is を使うケースがよく見られます。

D. People
この People の前には there's が省略されています。

E. all
この all は「完全に」という意味で、alone を強調する働きをしています。

F. Try not to
to 不定詞の否定形はこのように〈not to −〉という形を取ります。〈try not to 〉−で「−しないようにする」という意味です。

G. what is real
この what は先行詞 the thing(s) を含む関係代名詞で、この部分は the thing which is real というように書き換えることができ、「現実であるもの」という意味です。

H. No matter how hard we try
〈no matter how 副詞 S V〉で、「どれ程〜 S が V しても」という意味になるので、ここは「どれほど一生懸命私達が頑張っても」という意味になります。。

▶ SONG #7 Take A Step Back

I. The trials of a boy and a girl
　頭に These are が省略されています。その These はこの歌詞の中、さらには、このアルバム全体で言われている様々な困難な状況のことを指しています。

J. The world of a boy and a girl
　頭に This is が省略されています。その This はこの歌詞、さらには、このアルバム全体の中で言われている、主人公と彼女を取り巻く状況のことを指しています。

III. 重要表現

① **in a slump**：不調で

▶活用例
W : You feeling any better?
M : No, I'm still kind of down.
W : I'm sorry to hear that. Anything I can do?
M : No, I'll get over it. Thanks, though. I'm just in a slump right now.

W：気分少しは良くなった？
M：いや、まだちょっと落ち込んでる。
W：それは気の毒ね。何か私にできることある？
M：ううん、なんとか乗り越えるよ。でも、ありがとう。今ちょっとスランプなだけだから。

*__down__：落ち込んでいる
*__get over__ 〜：〜を克服する

② **which way is up**：困難な状況から抜け出す方法

▶活用例
W : So many things have gone wrong recently.
M : Yeah, I heard you're having a lot of trouble at work.
W : It's unbelievable! These days, I don't even know which way is up.

W：最近、うまくいかないことがほんとに沢山あるの。
M：うん、仕事上で沢山トラブルを抱えているって聞いたけど。
W：信じられないくらいよ！ 近頃は、どうやってその状況から抜け出すのかさえわからないわ。

*__go wrong__：(物事が) うまくいかない

③ **be out of one's hands**：〜の手に負えない

▶活用例
W : Is Mary really getting fired?
M : Yeah, I'm afraid so.
W : Can't you do something about it?
M : I wish I could but it's out of my hands.

W：メアリーはほんとにクビになるの？
M：うん、残念だけどそうみたい。
W：何かあなたにできることはないの？
M：何かできたらいいんだけど、僕の力の及ぶところじゃなくて。

*__get fired__：解雇される
*__I wish I could 〜.__：〜できたらいいのに

▶ SONG #7　Take A Step Back

④ go according to plan：計画通りにいく

▶活用例
W : How was your date? Tell me all about it!
M : Well, actually, things didn't go according to plan.
W : Oh no! What happened?
M : First the restaurant made a mistake with our reservation, so we had to find another place, then…

W：デートはどうだった？　全部聞かせてよ！
M：まぁ、実は計画通りにはいかなかったんだ。
W：ぇぇ！　何があったの？
M：まず、レストランが僕達の予約を間違えちゃっていたから、他のお店を探さなくちゃならなくなって、それから……

⑤ get in one's way：〜の邪魔をする

▶活用例
W : Did you end up going hiking on Saturday?
M : Yeah, but it was really crowded.
W : Oh, that's too bad.
M : Yeah, and I hike pretty fast so everybody just kept getting in my way.

W：土曜日は結局ハイキングに行くことになったの？
M：うん、でもものすごく混んでいたんだ。
W：それは残念だったわね。
M：うん、しかも、僕は結構早く歩くから、みんな邪魔でさあ。

⑥ ruin one's day：〜の一日を台無しにする

▶活用例
M : I can't believe Mark said those things to you.
W : Me, either. It totally ruined my day.
M : Well, why don't we get even with him? I have an idea how we can make him pay.

M：マークが君にそんなことを言ったなんて信じられない。
W：私も信じられないわ。ほんとにその日一日台無しだったわ。
M：じゃあ、彼に仕返ししちゃわない？　彼に思い知らせるアイデアがあるんだけど。

*get even with 〜：〜に仕返しする

⑦ make it through 〜：〜を何とか切り抜ける

▶活用例
W : I can't believe how many things I have to do!
M : Yeah, you seem pretty busy.
W : It's too much! I don't know if I can even make it through the day!

W：こんなに沢山やらなくちゃならないことがあるなんて、信じられないわ！
M：うん、かなり忙しそうだよね。
W：多過ぎだわ！　今日一日を乗り切れるかどうかもわかんない！

⑧ big picture：全体像、大局

▶活用例
M : Paul has been asking me all kinds of really detailed questions about our project.
W : Oh, he always does that.
M : Well, of course the details are important, but he focuses on them too much.
W : Yeah, I know. He never seems to see the big picture.

M：ポールが、僕達のプロジェクトについて、ありとあらゆる細かい質問をしてくるんだ。
W：ああ、彼はいつもそうよ。
M：うん、もちろん細かい点も重要だけど、彼はそういった点にこだわり過ぎるんだよね。
W：ええ、そうね。決して全体像を見てない感じよね。

*focus on 〜：〜に重点的に取り組む

⑨ It's no big deal.：大したことないよ

▶活用例
M : I'm sorry I broke your wine glass. Was it expensive?
W : Nah, not at all. I got it at the dollar shop.
M : Well, I still feel bad. I'll buy you a new one.
W : You don't have to do that. Really, it's no big deal.

M：君のワイングラスを割っちゃってゴメンね。高かった？
W：ううん、全然。1ドルショップで買ったの。
M：うーん、それでも気がとがめるなあ。新しいのを買うよ。
W：そんなことしなくていいわ。ほんとに、大したことないんだから。

SONG #7　Take A Step Back

⑩ lose track of ～：～を見失う、～の現状がわからなくなる

▶活用例
W : Did you invite Ann to the party?
M : Oh no! I completely forgot!
W : Really? Well, let's send her an invitation right now.
M : Yeah. Let's do that. I guess I just lost track of who I invited.

W：アンはパーティに呼んだの？
M：あっ、やばい！　完全に忘れてた！
W：ほんとに？　じゃあ、今すぐ招待状を送りましょうよ。
M：うん、そうしよう。僕は誰を招待したかわからなくなっちゃったみたいだ。

⑪ see eye to eye：意見が一致する

▶活用例
W : I really don't think we should rearrange the office.
M : Me, either. But if it's what Paul wants, we've gotta do it.
W : Yeah, I know. But I just disagree with so many of his ideas.
M : Me, too. We almost never see eye to eye.

W：このオフィスを模様替えすべきじゃないとほんとに思うんだけど。
M：僕もそう思うよ。でももしポールがそうしたいなら、僕達はそうするしかないんじゃない。
W：うん、わかってる。でも私はほんとに彼の案には反対なことが多いわ。
M：僕もだよ。ほとんど意見が一致することがないくらいだ。

⑫ end up －ing：結局―することになる
　get ～ across：～を伝える、～を理解させる
　tune ～ out：～に興味を示さない、～を無視する

▶活用例
W : Did anything interesting happen in the meeting?
M : Nope, boring as usual.
W : What did Paul say?
M : Nothing much. You know, he takes so long to get a point across that I usually just end up tuning him out.

W：何かミーティングで面白いことあった？
M：ぜんぜん。いつもの通り、退屈だったよ。
W：ポールは何て言ってたの？
M：たいしたことは言ってなかったなあ。まぁわかっているとは思うけど、彼は要点を言うまでがものすごく長いから、僕はたいてい結局は興味を失っちゃうんだよね。

*as usual：いつもの通り
*so ～ that S V：とても～なので S は V する

⑬ break one's heart：～を悲嘆にくれさせる

▶活用例
M : Jeff and Amy had another fight yesterday.
W : Oh no. What was it about this time?
M : Oh, the usual. She got upset at him about something or other, then he got mad and started tearing her apart.
W : Oh, it breaks my heart to hear that.

M：ジェフとエイミーは、また昨日喧嘩したんだよ。
W：やだ。今度は何が原因なの？
M：いつもと同じだよ。彼女が何かのことで彼に対して怒って、そうすると彼も怒って、彼女をけなし始めたんだ。
W：あぁ、そんなこと聞くと胸が張り裂けそうだわ。

*something or other：何か

⑭ down and out：打ちのめされて、どん底で
It's not the end of the world.：この世の終わりなんかじゃない
ups and downs：浮き沈み

▶活用例
M : Hey, I heard you and Jeff had another fight. You OK?
W : Yeah, I guess. But we've been fighting a lot recently.
M : That's no fun.
W : Yeah, these days, I'm just really down and out most of the time.
M : I know how you feel, but it's not the end of the world. Things could still get better.
W : That's true. We all have our ups and downs.

M：ねぇ、君とジェフがまた喧嘩したって聞いたんだけど。大丈夫？
W：うん、たぶんね。でも最近よく喧嘩しているのよね。
M：それはよくないね。
W：うん、近頃は、たいていほんとにどん底。
M：君の気持ちわかるよ。でもこの世の終わりってわけじゃないんだから。状況が良くなることだってあるよ。
W：その通りね。誰にだって浮き沈みがあるものね。

SONG #8
Don't Give Up

▶ SONG #8
Don't Give Up

(Verse 1)
Now that things are back to normal,
Everything is back on track,
I can catch my breath and relax.
It's been such a long, long time.
Finally a chance to unwind.

We got back together.
We kissed and made up.
I think we'll be OK even if something else comes up.
We may not be in the clear,
But for now there won't be as many tears.

(Chorus 1)
Sometimes we need some room to breathe,
To let things settle down,
To get our feet back on the ground.
But I believe in you and me.
That we can work it out,
Without a doubt.

(Verse 2)
My old life is history.
A thing of the past.
Of course it keeps changing, but now not so fast.
And as a new rule of thumb,
I'll deal with things as they come.

Sometimes unexpected things,
Catch us off guard.
And knowing what to do can often be hard.
Sometimes we have to make a stand.
Sometimes we have to take a chance.

(Chorus 2)
Sometimes we need to simply believe,
That everything is happening,
Exactly as it should.
Sometimes we need just to believe,
That everything happens for a reason.

(Bridge)
And it all comes down to communication.

(Ending)
Sometimes the wires get crossed.
Sometimes your point gets lost.

Maybe you didn't make sense.
Maybe you were too intense.

Maybe you said too much,
Or packed too much punch.

Maybe you tried too hard,
Or took it a little too far.

Maybe it wasn't crystal-clear.
Or maybe you just didn't hear.

But whatever the cause,
Whatever it was,
Sometimes communication falls through.
What can you do?

You have to let it slide.
Then give it another try.

Just don't give up. Don't give up. Don't give up.
Just give it another try.
Give it another try.
Just one more try.

Give it another try.
Just don't give up.
Just don't give up.
Don't give up.
Just give it one more try.
Give it one more try.
Just don't give up.

(Verse 1)
状況が元に戻って
すべてが復活したから
一息ついて　リラックスできる
ものすごく久しぶり
やっと訪れたリラックスの時

僕達は元どおり
キスをして　仲直りしたね
また何かが起きても　もう大丈夫
問題がすべて片付いたわけじゃないかもしれないけど
前ほどたくさんの涙が流れることは　当分ないだろう

(Chorus 1)
一息つくことも時には必要
物事を落ち着かせ
元の二人に戻るには
でも僕は二人を信じている
僕達はうまくやっていけるって
間違いない

(Verse 2)
今までの生活はもう過去のもの
過ぎ去った日々
もちろん生活は変わり続けているけれど　もっとゆったり変わっていく
今回の経験から決めたんだ
事が起きたら対処する

時々　思いもよらないことが
不意を突いて襲ってくる
何をすべきかわからないときもしばしば
抵抗しなくちゃならない時もある
いちかばちかに賭けなきゃならないこともある

(Chorus 2)
時にはこう信じることが必要
すべてのことは起こるもの
まさに　起こるべくして
また　時にはこう信じることも必要
すべての出来事には理由があるのだと

(Bridge)
結局　すべてはコミュニケーション

(Ending)
時々　誤解することがある
時々　言いたいことがわからなくなる

話の筋が通っていなかったのかもしれないし
言うことが強烈すぎたのかもしれない

言いすぎたのかもしれないし
言葉が強すぎたのかもしれない

たぶん張り切りすぎたのか
ちょっと行きすぎたのだろう

言葉がはっきりしていなかったか
ただ聞き漏らしただけかもしれない

でも理由が何であれ
それが何であれ
コミュニケーションがうまくいかない時はあるものだ
その時何が出来るというのだろう

そんな時は　ただ成り行きに任せ
時がきたら　もう一度トライしてみる

とにかく諦めちゃダメ　諦めちゃダメ　諦めちゃダメ
もう一度トライしてみて
もう一度トライして
とにかくもう一度だけ

もう一度トライして
とにかく諦めないで
とにかく諦めないで
諦めないで
とにかくもう一度トライして
もう一度トライして
とにかく諦めないで

SONG #8　Don't Give Up

曲解説

　アルバムの最後を飾るこの曲では、レイドバックしたレゲエ風のリズムに優しいメロディーが乗り、アルバム全体を締めくくるテーマが歌い上げられます。

　オルガンの音と共に曲がフェードインしてくると、まず最初に、状況が元に戻ったことで主人公が一息ついていることが示されます（**Now that things are back to normal, everything is back on track, I can catch my breath and relax.**）。二人もキスをして、仲直りしたのです（**We kissed and made up.**）。

　主人公は、今回の経験から、一人で先走るのではなく、事が起きたら対処するという人生哲学を得ます（**And as a new rule of thumb, I'll deal with things as they come.**）。さらに、全ては理由があって起きるのだとも悟ります（**Sometimes we need just to believe that everything happens for a reason.**）。

　そして出てくる次の一文が、このアルバムを通してジェフが一番伝えたかったテーマです。**And it all comes down to communication.**　結局全てはコミュニケーション。5曲目で、主人公が言った言葉を覚えていらっしゃるでしょうか？　**I don't understand you anyway. You never ever make any sense!**　そう、実は二人の間が上手くいかなくなったのも、コミュニケーションが上手くいかなくなったことが原因だったのです。

　ジェフは、人間関係の基本はコミュニケーションであり、皆が努力して、より良いコミュニケーションを築き上げることが、スムーズな人間関係にとって欠くことのできない要素であるということを訴えたかったのです。

　しかし、様々な理由で、コミュニケーションが上手く取れないときは生じます。そんな時はどうしようもありません（**Sometimes communication falls through. What can you do?**）。

　ではどうするか？　そんな時は、ただ成り行きに任せ、時が来たら再度トライするのです（**You have to let it slide. Then give it another try.**）。

　とにかく諦めないで欲しい。もう一度トライして欲しい（**Just don't give up. Just give it another try.**）。こんな願いを主人公の口を通してジェフが何度も何度も訴える中、このアルバムは幕を閉じていきます。

I. 学習用歌詞

(Verse 1)
Now that things are back to normal, everything **is back on track**, I can **catch my**
1   2   3
breath and relax.
It's been such a long, long **time**.
4
Finally a chance to **unwind**.
           5

We got back together.
We kissed and **made up**.
              2
I think we'll be OK **even if** something else **comes up**.
                    6   7
We may not **be in the clear**, but for now there won't be as many tears.
            8   A

(Chorus 1)
Sometimes we need some **room to breathe** to let things **settle down**, to **get our**
                        9   5   10
feet back on the ground.
But I **believe in** you and me.
       11
That we can work it out, **without a doubt**.
B   11

(Verse 2)
My old life is **history**.
               12
A thing of the past.
Of course it keeps changing, but now not so fast.
And **as a** new **rule of thumb**, I'll **deal with** things as they come.
     13   14

Sometimes unexpected things **catch** us **off guard**.
                             15
And knowing what to do can often be hard.
    C
Sometimes we have to **make a stand**.
                     16
Sometimes we have to take a chance.

SONG #8   Don't Give Up

(Chorus 2)
Sometimes we need to simply believe that everything is happening exactly <u>as it</u>
                                                                                    D
<u>should</u>.
Sometimes we need just to believe that everything happens **for a reason**.
                                                                    17

(Bridge)
And **it all comes down to** communication.
      18

(Ending)
Sometimes **the wires get crossed**.
              19
Sometimes **your point gets lost**.
              E 20

Maybe you didn't make sense.
Maybe you were too intense.

Maybe you said too much, or **packed** too much **punch**.
                                 21

Maybe you tried too hard, or **took** it a little **too far**.
                                 21

Maybe it wasn't **crystal-clear**.
                  22
Or maybe you just didn't hear.

But whatever the cause, whatever it was, sometimes communication **falls through**.
       F   23
What can you do?
23

You have to **let it slide**.
              23
Then **give it another try**.
       24

Just don't **give up**.
             24

Don't give up.
Don't give up.
Just give it another try.
Give it another try.
Just one more try.

Give it another try.
Just don't give up.
Just don't give up.
Don't give up.
Just give it one more try.
Give it one more try.
Just don't give up.

▶SONG #8　Don't Give Up

Ⅱ. 語句解説

A. there won't be as many tears
　tears の後ろには as before のような語句が省略されています。「以前ほど多くの涙はないだろう」というのが直訳です。このように、〈as ～ as …〉を用いた原級比較において、2つ目の as 以降が省略されることがよくあります。このような場合は、文脈から省略された語句を推測します。省略されているということは、推測可能だから省略されているわけで、文脈から考えれば、省略された語句を推測することはそれ程難しいことではありません。

B. That
　この That の前には I believe という語句が省略されています。

C. knowing
　この knowing は動名詞で、「知ること」という意味になり、文の主語になっています。

D. as it should
　should の後ろには be happening が省略されています。またこの should は「当然－するはずだ」という意味で、この部分全体で「当然起こるように」という意味になっています。

E. your
　この your や、その後の歌詞の中で出てくる you は、主人公が彼女に向かって呼びかける you ではなく、一般の人全体を表す you です。物事を一般化して言う際に用いられます。

F. whatever the cause
　cause の後ろには was が省略されており、「原因が何であったとしても」という意味です。

III. 重要表現

① now that S V：今や S は V するので

▶活用例
W : Do you want to do anything this weekend?
M : Yeah, sure. What do you have in mind?
W : Well, now that we've gotten our bonuses, how about going shopping?
M : That sounds great!

W：今週末、何かしたい？
M：もちろん。君はどうしたい？
W：そうねー、ボーナスも出たことだし、買い物なんかどう？
M：いいねえ！

*How about -ing ?：―するのはどうですか？

② be back on track：元に戻っている
make up：仲直りする

▶活用例
W : Hey, I heard you and Amy were fighting.
M : Yeah, but we worked it out. Everything's alright now. We made up.
W : That's great. So, you're not going to call off the wedding?
M : Of course not! It's all back on track.

W：ねぇ、あなたとエイミーが喧嘩しているって聞いたけど。
M：うん、でも解決したよ。今はもう大丈夫。仲直りしたんだ。
W：それは良かったわ。じゃあ、結婚を取りやめたりはしないのね？
M：もちろんしないよ！　全て元通りさ。

*call off 〜：〜を取りやめる

③ catch one's breath：一息つく

▶活用例
W : Can you help me take these things out to the car?
M : Actually, do you mind if we do it later?
W : Not at all. That's no problem.
M : Thanks. I'm just so busy today. I haven't had a chance to catch my breath.

W：この辺のものを車まで運ぶのを手伝ってくれない？
M：うーん、後でじゃだめかなぁ？
W：全然かまわないわ。いいわよ。
M：ありがとう。今日はとにかく忙しくって。息つく暇もないんだ。

▶ SONG #8　Don't Give Up

④ It's been (such) a long time.：（すごく）久しぶりだ

▶活用例

M : Oh my gosh! Abby? Is that you?
W : Jeff? Wow! I can't believe it!
M : It's been such a long time!
W : It sure has. What have you been up to?

M：あれぇー！　アビー？　君なのかい？
W：ジェフ？　わぁー！　信じられない！
M：すごい久しぶりだね！
W：ほんとね。最近、何してたの？

*__What have you been up to?__：最近、何してたの？

⑤ unwind：緊張をほぐす
　settle down：落ち着く

▶活用例

W : I need a vacation.
M : Tell me about it. I can't wait for things to settle down.
W : Yeah. I'm so wound up.
M : Well, why don't we grab a beer after work and unwind a little bit?
W : That sounds good.

W：休暇が必要だわ。
M：全くだね。この忙しさが落ち着くのが待ち遠しいよ。
W：うん。もうほんとにイライラしちゃって。
M：じゃあ、仕事が終わったらビールでも飲みに行って、ちょっと緊張をほぐさない？
W：それはいいわね。

*__Tell me about it.__：その通りだ
*__can't wait for ～ to －__：～が—するのが待ち遠しい
*__be wound up__：苛立っている

⑥ even if S V：たとえ S が V しても

▶活用例
M : Do you want to go to the beach on Saturday?
W : Yeah, I'd love to! But, what if it's rainy?
M : Well, let's go even if it's rainy. We're going to get wet anyway!
W : That's true.

M：土曜日にビーチに行かない？
W：うん、行きたい！　でも、雨だったらどうするの？
M：そうだね、雨でも行こうよ。どっちにしても濡れるんだから！
W：確かに。

*get wet：濡れる

⑦ come up：（問題などが）発生する

▶活用例
W : Hello?
M : Hey Karen. It's James.
W : Hi James! What's going on?
M : Well, I'm sorry, but I'm not going to be able to make it to your party tonight. Something came up and I have to work late.

W：もしもし？
M：やあ、カレン。ジェームズだよ。
W：あぁ、ジェームズ！　どうしたの？
M：うーん、悪いんだけど、今夜の君のパーティに行けなくなっちゃったんだ。ちょっと問題が起きて、遅くまで働かなくちゃならないんだよ。

*What's going on?：どうしたの？
*make it to ～：～に出席する

⑧ be in the clear：危機を脱している

▶活用例
W : Did you get everything worked out with the boss?
M : Yeah, pretty much.
W : So, you're in the clear?
M : I think so, as long as I don't mess up again.

W：上司とは全て上手くいった？
M：うん、大体ね。
W：じゃあ、危機は脱したのね？
M：と思うよ。また失敗しない限りはね。

*get ～ worked out：～がうまくいく
*as long as S V：S が V する限りは
*mess up：失敗する

▶SONG #8 Don't Give Up

⑨ room to breathe：一息つく機会

▶活用例
M : Hey Amy, are you up for a beer tonight?
W : I don't know. I should maybe go home. Jeff is probably making dinner tonight.
M : Oh, come on. You two are always together. You need some room to breathe, right?
W : That's true. OK then. Let's have a drink.

M：ねえ、エイミー、今夜一緒にビールなんてどう？
W：どうかなあ。もしかしたら家に帰ったほうがいいかも。多分ジェフが今夜夕飯を作ってくれるから。
M：えー、いいじゃない。君達二人はいつも一緒なんだから。一息つくことも必要でしょ？
W：まあその通りね。じゃあ、わかったわ。飲みに行きましょう。

*Are you up for 〜？：〜に乗り気ですか？

⑩ get one's feet back on the ground：元の安定した状態に戻る

▶活用例
W : So, how's your new job?
M : It's going well. It's nice to have a regular income again.
W : Oh, I'm sure. You were having a rough time for a while.
M : Yeah. It feels good to finally get my feet back on the ground.

W：それで、新しい仕事はどう？
M：うまく行ってるよ。また定期的に収入が入るようになったのはいいことだね。
W：あー、そうでしょうね。しばらく大変な日が続いたもの。
M：うん。ようやく元に戻って、いい感じだね。

⑪ believe in 〜：〜（の力）を信頼する
without a doubt：疑いなく

▶活用例
W : Did you know that Dan's running for mayor?
M : Really? Wow! Do you think he'll win?
W : Oh, without a doubt! I completely believe in him.

W：ダンが市長に立候補するって知ってた？
M：ほんと？　わー！　彼、勝てると思う？
W：うん、もちろん！　彼なら勝てるって、完全に信じてるわ。

*run for 〜：〜に立候補する

⑫ history：過去のもの

▶活用例

M : Our paychecks are going to be a week late again.
W : What!? Again!? I can't believe this!
M : Me, either. This company's going down the tubes.
W : Yeah. I bet this company will be history by next month.

M：また給料が一週間遅れそうだよ。
W：なんですって！？ また！？ 信じられない！
M：全く。この会社、潰れるんじゃない。
W：うん。きっと来月までには、この会社、過去のものになっているわよ。

*go down the tubes：駄目になる
*I bet S V .：きっと S は V する

⑬ as a rule of thumb：経験からいって、指針として

▶活用例

M : Well, what happened?
W : He's a really nice guy! And, I got his phone number!
M : See? I told you that you should talk to him.
W : You were right. And from now on, as a rule of thumb, I'm not going to be so shy anymore.

M：さてと、それでどうなったの？
W：彼は、ほんとにいい人ね！ で、彼の電話番号を教えてもらっちゃった！
M：でしょ？ 言ったじゃない、彼と話したほうがいいって。
W：あなたの言う通りだったわね。これからは、経験からいって、もうあまり恥ずかしがらないようにするわ。

⑭ deal with 〜：〜に対処する、〜を扱う

▶活用例

W : Hey Jeff, your customer, Mr. Thorne, is on the phone and he's really upset.
M : Again? What is it this time?
W : I don't know, but he's pretty angry.
M : OK, let me talk to him. I'll deal with it.

W：ねえ、ジェフ。あなたのお客さんのソーンさんから電話なんだけど、ほんとに怒ってるわよ。
M：また？ 今度は何？
W：わからないわ。でも、かなり怒ってるわよ。
M：わかった、僕が出るよ。僕が処理する。

SONG #8　Don't Give Up

⑮ catch 〜 off guard：〜の不意を衝く

▶活用例
W : You look like you just saw a ghost! You OK?
M : I just got promoted to area manager.
W : Really? Well, isn't that a good thing?
M : Yeah, it is. I guess it just really caught me off guard.

W：お化けを見たような顔してるけど！　大丈夫？
M：たった今、エリア マネジャーに昇進したんだ。
W：ほんとに？　えーと、それはいいことなんじゃないの？
M：うん、そうなんだけど。ほんとに不意を衝かれた感じで。

*get promoted：昇進する

⑯ make a stand：抵抗する

▶活用例
W : I can't believe we have another company party on Friday.
M : Me, either. This has been happening too much recently.
W : Why don't we tell the boss we're tired of it and we're not going?
M : Yeah, we should. Somebody has to make a stand.

W：金曜日に、また別の社内パーティがあるなんて信じられないわ。
M：同感。最近ちょっと多過ぎるよね。
W：もううんざりしてるから行かないって、上司に言わない？
M：うん、言うべきだよね。誰かが反対しないとね。

⑰ for a reason：理由があって

▶活用例
W : Do you remember that I lost my wallet last week?
M : Yeah, of course.
W : Well, this morning I got it back. And, the guy who found it was really nice! We're having dinner together tonight.
M : No way! It's so interesting how things sometimes work out. I guess you lost your wallet for a reason.

W：先週、私が財布をなくしたの覚えてる？
M：うん、もちろん。
W：それでね、今朝戻ってきたの。その上、財布を見つけてくれた人が、ほんとに素敵な人だったのよ！　今夜一緒に食事するの。
M：まさか！　時々物事がうまく行くのって、ほんとに面白いよね。財布をなくしたのにも、訳があったというわけだね。

⑱ It all comes down to ～ .：（問題は全て）結局～ということになる、～が一番大事ということになる

▶活用例
W : So, what was Mr. Thorne upset about this time?
M : Oh, I made a small mistake with his order.
W : Ah, I see. You know, you work really hard, but sometimes what you say isn't perfectly clear.
M : Yeah, you're right.
W : Remember, it all comes down to communication.

W：それで、ソーンさんは今度は何のことで怒ってたの？
M：あー、彼の注文に関して、僕がちょっとしたミスをしたんだ。
W：あー、なるほど。ほら、あなたはほんとに一生懸働くけど、時々言ってることがはっきりしないじゃない。
M：うん、そうだね。
W：いい、全てはコミュニケーションなの。

⑲ The wires get crossed.：誤解が生じる

▶活用例
W : I was supposed to meet Mary this morning, but she didn't show up.
M : Again? That happens pretty often with her, huh?
W : Yeah, somehow the wires get crossed and we end up miscommunicating.

W：今朝メアリーと会うはずだったんだけど、彼女来なかったの。
M：また？　彼女とは、よくそういうことがあるよねぇ？
W：うん、なぜか誤解が生じて、結局話が上手く伝わらないってことになっちゃうのよね。

*be supposed to ー：ーすることになっている
*show up：現れる

⑳ One's point gets lost.：～の言いたいことがわからない

▶活用例
W : So anyway, as I was saying, I really think we should…
M : Sorry, did you just say something about going out tomorrow?
W : Well, yeah, a minute ago, but anyway, I think we should…
M : Well then, let's go out tomorrow! And, what else were you saying?
W : You know, forget it. Every time I talk to you, my point gets lost.

W：まあとにかく、さっき私が言ってたように、ほんとに私達はすべきだと思うの・・・
M：ごめん、なにか明日出かけるとかなんとか言った？
W：えっと、うん、一分ぐらい前に、まあでも、私が思うに、私達は・・・

▶ SONG #8   Don't Give Up

M：そしたら、明日出かけようよ！　えーと、他に何言ってたっけ？
W：まあ、もういいわよ。あなたに話すたびに、言いたいことがわからなくなっちゃうわ。

㉑ **pack a punch**：威力がある、強い影響を及ぼす
　 take 〜 too far：〜をやり過ぎる

▶活用例
M : That movie was pretty intense, huh?
W : Yeah, it sure packed a punch.
M : Do you think they took the action scenes a little too far, though?
W : Yeah, some of them were too much.

M：あの映画はかなり強烈だったよね？
W：うん、とにかくすごいパンチが効いてたわね。
M：でもアクションシーンはちょっとやり過ぎじゃなかった？
W：そうね、行き過ぎのところもあったわね。

㉒ **crystal-clear**：非常に明瞭な

▶活用例
W : Did you get that email from Simon?
M : Yeah, but I couldn't understand anything he wrote.
W : Me, either. It definitely wasn't crystal-clear.
M : No kidding. He was probably drinking when he wrote it.

W：サイモンからのメール届いた？
M：うん、でも彼が書いていることは全然理解できなかったよ。
W：私もよ。確かに明確ではなかったわね。
M：ほんとにそうだね。書いてた時、たぶん飲んでたんだよ。

㉓ **fall through**：失敗に終わる
　 What can you do?：どうしようもない
　 let it slide：成り行きにまかせる

▶活用例
W : Are you all still planning to visit Europe this summer?
M : Actually, no. Everyone had some problem either with the airfare or timing or whatever. So, the whole plan fell through.
W : Oh, that's too bad.
M : Well, what can you do? Got to let it slide this time.

W：この夏、まだヨーロッパに行く予定でいるの？
M：実はやめたんだ。みんな、飛行機代やスケジュールなんかのことで問題があってね。だから計画は全部だめになっちゃったんだよ。
W：あら、それは残念だったわね。

M：うーん、でもどうしようもないよね。今回はそうするしかないや。

㉔ give it another try：もう一度やってみる
　　give up：諦める

> ▶活用例
> W : I really don't know if I can do it.
> M : Oh, I'm sure you can. Just give it another try.
> W : But I've already tried so many times!
> M : I know. But don't give up! I'm sure you can do it.

W：私にできるかどうか、ほんとにわからないわ。
M：あー、君ならきっとできるよ。とにかくもう一度やってごらんよ。
W：でももう何度もトライしてるのよ！
M：わかってる。だけど諦めちゃだめだよ！　きっとできるってば。

INDEX

Song#	対話番号	*	表現	意味
1	1		have got butterflies in one's stomach	（緊張して）ドキドキする、そわそわする
1	1	*	freaked out	パニック状態に陥っている
1	1	*	What's up?	どうしたの？　最近調子はどう？
1	2		One's heart skips a beat.	心臓がドキッとする
1	2	*	Oh my god!	何てことだ！　信じられない！　まあ！
1	2	*	get hit by ~	～に轢かれる
1	2	*	No way!	まさか！
1	3		be swept off one's feet	（誰かに）夢中になる
1	4		One's head is in the clouds.	夢想にふけって集中できない
1	4		I guess S V.	S は V すると思う
1	4	*	kind of	ちょっと、なんだか
1	4	*	out of it	ぼーっとして
1	4	*	have ~ on one's mind	～を気にかけている
1	5		take ~ out for …	～を…に連れ出す
1	5		night on the town	夜の街で楽しむこと
1	5		shoot the breeze	おしゃべりする
1	6		cruise around	あちこち回る
1	7		Anything is fine with ~ .	～にとっては何でも構わない
1	7		hang out	時を過ごす、一緒にいる、ブラブラする
1	8		kick back	のんびりする
1	8	*	Do you mind if S V?	S が V してもいいですか？
1	9		be crazy about ~	～に夢中になっている
1	9		fall head over heels	完全に恋に落ちる
1	9		every time S V	S が V するたびに
1	9		One's knees get weak.	（緊張して）膝がガクガクする
1	9	*	Sounds like S V.	〈話を聞いていると〉 S は V するようだ
1	9	*	fall for ~	～に恋する
1	10		too ~ to ―	～過ぎて―できない
1	11		be in seventh heaven	本当に幸せである
1	11		float on cloud nine	夢見心地である
1	11	*	It feels ~ to ―.	―するのは～に感じられる
1	12		in no time	すぐに
1	12	*	be on one's way	向かっているところだ
1	13		What's new?	最近、何かあった？

Song#	対話番号	*	表現	意味
1	13		How's it going?	最近どう？
1	13	*	not bad	まあまあ良い
1	14		~ will do.	～で大丈夫
1	14	*	Just a sec.	ちょっと待って
1	15		would rather －	むしろ―したい、―するほうがいい
1	15	*	Feel like － ing?	―する？、―したい気分？
1	15	*	go out for a drink	飲みに行く
1	16		push ~ away from …	～を…から追いやる
1	17		rush things	慌てて物事を行う
1	18		be in one's shoes	～と同じ立場に身を置く
1	18		put it out there	隠さずに全て話す
1	18	*	Why don't you － ?	―したらどうですか？
1	18	*	what S V	S が V すること
1	19		take a chance	いちかばちかやってみる
1	19	*	audition for ~	～のオーディションを受ける
1	19	*	Why not?	どうして（しないの）？
1	19	*	You never know.	先のことはわからないよ
1	19	*	Come on.	さあさあ
1	20		wait and see	成り行きを見守る
1	20	*	be sold out	売り切れだ
1	20	*	be good at － ing	―するのが得意だ
1	21		one of these days	いつかそのうち
1	21	*	be gonna －	―するだろう、―するつもりだ
1	21	*	quit － ing	―するのをやめる
1	21	*	hold one's breath	期待して待つ
1	22		spill one's guts	全て話す
1	22		gather up one's courage	勇気を奮い起こす
1	23		think it through	とことん考える
1	23	*	picky	好みがうるさい
1	24		once S V	ひとたび S が V すると
1	25		be out in the open	明るみに出る
1	25	*	admit to － ing	―したことを認める
1	25	*	I knew it!	やっぱり！　それみたことか！
1	26		take it back	取り消す

INDEX

Song#	対話番号	*	表現	意味
1	26	*	feel bad	後悔する、気がとがめる
1	27		kill ~	~にひどい苦痛を与える
1	28		worth a try	試すだけの価値がある
1	28	*	go haywire	おかしくなる、狂う
1	28	*	take a look at ~	~を見る
1	29		something along the lines of ~	~のようなこと
1	30		Why don't we ー ?	ーしませんか？
1	30	*	be in the mood for ~	~を食べたい気分だ、~をしたい気分だ
2	1		fat paycheck	多額の給料
2	1	*	seem to ー	ーするようだ
2	2		run dry	空になる、なくなる
2	3		kick ass	【卑】凄いことをする、迫力満点だ、徹底的に楽しむ
2	3	*	~ , huh?	~でしょ？
2	4		take a break	一休みする
2	4		put one's feet up	（座って）休む、リラックスする
2	5		get some sleep	眠る
2	5		take it slow	のんきにやる、リラックスする
2	5	*	like	だいたい
2	6		which is which	どっちがどっちか
2	6	*	would love to ー	ぜひーしたい
2	6	*	can't tell	わからない
2	7		lose one's shit	【卑】頭がおかしくなる
2	8		out of the blue	突然
2	8	*	get cut loose	リストラされる
2	9		jones for ~	~が欲しくてたまらない、~したくてたまらない
2	9	*	freak out	パニックに陥る、気がおかしくなる
2	9	*	What's wrong with you?	どうしたの？
2	9	*	bad	ひどく
2	10		have got to ー	ーしなければならない
2	10	*	Oh, no!	しまった！
2	11		get out of ~	~から出る
2	11	*	be bushed	へとへとに疲れている

Song#	対話番号	*	表現	意味
2	12		have got nowhere to go	行く所がない
2	12	*	Any chance SV?	SがVする可能性はありますか？
2	12	*	crash at ~	~に急に泊めてもらう
2	13		cut down on ~	~を減らす
2	14		get one's shit together	【卑】きちんとやる、元のきちんとした自分に戻る
2	14		get on the ball	きちんとやる、気を引き締める
2	15		lose it	自制心を失う、キレる、おかしくなる
2	15		crack	神経がおかしくなる、だめになる
2	15		mess	混乱、滅茶苦茶な様子、滅茶苦茶な人
2	16		No joke.	冗談じゃない
2	16	*	mess with ~	~をからかう
2	17		It's not just that S V.	ただSがVするということだけではない
2	17	*	stand	我慢する
2	17	*	listen to ~ ー	~がーするのを聞く
2	18		lounge around	ダラダラ過ごす
2	18	*	get ~ off	~休みを取る
2	18	*	be up to ~	~をする、~しようと計画する
2	19		make something of oneself	頑張って成功する、立身出世する
2	20		do something about ~	~をどうにかする
2	20	*	Looks like S V.	SはVするようだ
2	20	*	hold on	待つ
2	21		get it off one's chest	心の内を明かす
2	21		lay it out for ~	~に細かく話す
2	21	*	bug	いらいらさせる
2	21	*	Go on and ー.	どうぞーしてください
3	1		S feel like S V.	SはVするように感じる
3	1	*	Man.	うわぁ
3	2		hustle and bustle	喧騒
3	2		daily grind	日課
3	2	*	wear ~ out	~を疲れさせる
3	2	*	day in and day out	毎日毎日
3	2	*	I know what you mean.	君の言いたいことわかるよ
3	3		be in one's own little world	自分だけの小さな世界の中にいる

INDEX

Song#	対話番号	*	表現	意味
3	4		mean it	本気だ、本気で言っている
3	4	*	you know	~でしょ、ご存知の通り、あのね、えーと
3	5		for once	今度だけは
3	5		more than enough ~	十分過ぎる~
3	5	*	take off	すぐに出る
3	6		get up on the right/wrong side of the bed	起きた時から機嫌がいい / 悪い
3	6	*	as far as S V	S が V する限りは
3	7		clear one's head	頭をすっきりさせる
3	7	*	drive ~ mad	~を怒らせる
3	7	*	work on ~	~に従事する
3	8		fall into place	上手くいく
3	8		click	しっくりいく
3	8	*	like clockwork	正確に
3	9		vanish without a trace	跡形もなく消える
3	10		stare out into space	宙をじっと見つめる
3	10		be on one's mind	気にかかっている、考えている
3	10	*	I should have known.	気が付かなかったが当然そうだ
3	11		as ~ as can be	この上なく~
3	11	*	Same here.	全く同感だ
3	12		wipe the smile off of one's face	ニヤニヤ笑いをやめる
3	13		time to spare	余った時間、自由に使える時間
3	13	*	come together	まとまる
3	14		get stuck in traffic	渋滞にはまる
3	15		grab a cuppa joe	コーヒーを 1 杯飲む
3	15		grab a bite	軽い食事をする
3	16		at one's own pace	~自身のペースで
3	17		catch a glimpse of ~	~をちょっと見る
3	17	*	go see	見に行く
3	17	*	call in sick	病欠の電話を入れる
3	18		out of sight	とてつもない、素晴らしい
3	18	*	be written all over one's face	顔に書いてある
3	19		be on the verge of ~	~寸前だ
3	20		clean oneself up	身なりを整える
3	20		scrounge up ~	(探し回って) ~を手に入れる

Song#	対話番号	＊	表現	意味
3	20	*	I'll see what I can do.	なんとかしてみるよ、できるだけやってみるよ
3	21		finish off	（飲食物を）平らげる
3	21	*	call it a night	今夜はこれで終わりにする
3	22		be meant to －	－するよう運命づけられている
4	1		in the blink of an eye	一瞬のうちに
4	2		have a grip on ~	~を把握する
4	2		have got it all figured out	全て把握している、何をどうすべきか全てわかっている
4	2	*	S look like S V.	S は V するようだ
4	2	*	be in a world of mess	大きな問題を抱えている
4	3		slip by ~	~の頭から抜け落ちる
4	3	*	forget to －	－するのを忘れる
4	4		haven't got a clue	わからない
4	5		any way you look at it	どう見ても
4	6		be blocked at every turn	いたる所で行き詰っている
4	6	*	no matter what S V	何を S が V しても
4	7		be about to －	まさに－しようとしている
4	7	*	make a phone call	電話する
4	7	*	have ~ －	~に－してもらう
4	8		crash and burn	おじゃんになる、大失敗する
4	9		go smoothly	うまくいく
4	9	*	Long time no see.	久しぶり
4	9	*	How have you been?	元気でやってた？
4	10		turn ~ around	~をひっくり返す
4	10	*	What about it?	それがどうかしたの？
4	11		fall behind ~	~から遅れる
4	11	*	as it is	もうすでに
4	12		be on the block	なくなる危機に瀕している
4	13		be on edge	極限状態にいる、ピリピリしている、不安だ
4	13	*	take it easy	気楽にやる
4	14		pull it off	うまくやる
4	14	*	close a deal with ~	~との商談をまとめる

INDEX

Song#	対話番号	*	表現	意味
4	15		give it one's best	全力を尽くしてやる
4	15	*	take over ~	~を引き継ぐ
4	16		cut ~ loose	~を切り捨てる、~を解雇する
4	16		let ~ go	~を手放す、~を解雇する
4	16		get laid off	リストラされる
4	16	*	cut back	削減する
4	17		get to ~	~を苦しめる、~に効く、~に到達する
4	18		as if S V	まるでSがVするかのように
4	19		go from bad to worse	ますます悪化する
4	19	*	turn into ~	~に変わる
4	20		fall apart	バラバラになる、崩壊する
4	20	*	~, right?	~ですよね？
4	20	*	It seems like S V.	SはVするようだ
4	21		go down the drain	失敗に終わる
4	21	*	start from scratch	最初からやり直す
4	21	*	in the world	一体全体
4	21	*	go ahead	先に進む
4	21	*	as planned	計画通りに
4	22		as for ~	~に関しては
4	23		see	交際する
4	23	*	go out with ~	~と交際する
4	23	*	What do you see in ~ ?	~のどこがいいの？
4	23	*	Good question.	いい質問だ
5	1		Forget it.	もういいよ
5	1	*	Can you do me a favor?	お願いがあるんだけど
5	1	*	Hold on a sec.	ちょっと待って
5	1	*	take care of ~	~を処理する
5	2		get it	理解する
5	2		make sense	意味をなす、道理にかなう
5	2	*	except for ~	~を除いて
5	2	*	go over ~	~を説明する
5	3		don't buy it	信じない
5	3		see through ~	~の正体を見抜く
5	3		call it quits	終わりにする

Song#	対話番号	*	表現	意味
5	4		get it over with	けりをつける、終わりにする
5	4	*	way around ~	~を回避する方法
5	4	*	might as well ―	―したほうがいい
5	5		be through with ~	~を終えている
5	5	*	be done	終わった、完了した
5	6		can't take any more of ~	~にはもう我慢の限界だ
5	6	*	go crazy	気が狂う
5	6	*	all the time	いつも
5	7		have had it up to here	これ以上我慢できない
5	7	*	break up	別れる
5	7	*	How dare S ― ?	よくもSは―できるものだ
5	7	*	work ~ out	~をなんとか解決する
5	8		Go on!	出て行け！
5	8		Get out!	消えうせろ！
5	8	*	How could S ― ?	よくもSは―できたものだ
5	8	*	be out of one's mind	気が狂っている
5	9		snap	感情をぶちまける、キレる
5	9		drop it	（議論などを）やめる
5	9	*	shouldn't have p.p.	―すべきではなかったのに（してしまった）
5	10		That's it.	それで終わりだ、ただそれだけ
5	10		go talk to ~	~に話しに行く
5	11		leave ~ alone	~をそっとしておく
5	12		on one's own	一人で、自力で
5	13		get on with it	やるべきことを急いでやり始める
5	13	*	be in the mood to ―	―する気になっている
5	14		handle	対処する、行う、耐える
5	15		Do me a favor and ―.	お願いだから―してください
5	16		get out of one's face	~の前から去る
5	16	*	be on one's case	~にうるさくしてくる
5	16	*	be stressed out	イライラしている
5	17		get off one's case	~にうるさく言わない、~をそっとしておく
5	17	*	do the laundry	洗濯する
5	17	*	be busy ― ing	―するのに忙しい

INDEX

Song#	対話番号	*	表現	意味
5	18		take one's place	～の代わりをする、～の後任になる
5	18	*	no problem	構わない、大丈夫
5	19		tear ~ apart	～の心を引き裂く、～を苦しめる、～をけなす
5	19	*	be sorry to hear ~	～を聞いて気の毒に思う
5	20		It's about time for ~ to －.	そろそろ～が－してもいい頃だ、そろそろ～が－する時間だ
5	21		Come off it.	馬鹿なことを言うな、嘘をつくな
5	22		budge an inch	譲る
5	22		What if S V ?	もし S が V したとしたらどうなるだろう？
5	22	*	no use	無駄な
5	23		Screw it.	【卑】もう駄目だ、もういいよ
5	24		blow it	台無しにする、しくじる
5	24	*	freeze	（コンピューターが）フリーズする
5	24	*	get the picture	状況を理解する
5	25		get away with it	罰せられずにやりおおせる、処罰をのがれる
5	25	*	go to jail	収監される
5	25	*	because of ~	～のせいで
5	26		pay for ~	～の償いをする、～の報いを受ける
5	26	*	sentence ~ to …years	～に懲役…年の判決を言い渡す
5	27		You know what?	あのね、いいかい
5	27	*	have trouble －ing	－するのに苦労する
6	1		mean to －	－するつもりだ
6	2		go overboard	極端に走る、夢中にやる
6	2	*	put ~ together	～を企画する
6	3		be out of one's head	頭がどうかしている
6	3	*	not really	そうでもない
6	3	*	pretty much	けっこう、ほとんど
6	4		lose control	自制心を失う、カッとなる
6	4	*	go drinking with ~	～と飲みに行く
6	4	*	yell at ~	～を怒鳴りつける
6	5		get out of line	間違ったことをやり過ぎる
6	5	*	No kidding.	冗談じゃない、全くその通りだ

Song#	対話番号	*	表現	意味
6	6		All S can do is －．	Sにできるのは－することだけだ
6	6	*	send off ~	~を発送する
6	6	*	get into ~	~に入学する
6	7		make it up to ~	~に償いをする
6	8		blow one's stack	キレる
6	9		push one's buttons	人の嫌がることをわざとする
6	9	*	over and over again	何度も何度も
6	9	*	keep － ing	－し続ける
6	10		It's one's fault.	~のせいだ
6	10		be to blame	責めを負うべきだ
6	10		flip out	カッとなる
6	10	*	let it go	それを忘れる
6	10	*	get back to normal	元に戻る
6	11		jerk	馬鹿者、むかつく奴
6	11	*	have a fight	喧嘩する
6	11	*	I'm sure S V.	きっとSはVする
6	12		patch things up	仲直りする
6	12	*	miss ~	~がいなくて寂しいと思う
6	12	*	get back together	よりを戻す
6	13		make ~ work	~がうまく行くようにする
6	13	*	fix	元の状態に戻す
6	14		if S V	SがVするかどうか
6	15		be scared of － ing	－するのが怖い
6	16		I'm afraid S V.	（残念ながら）SはVすると思う
6	16	*	Can I talk to ~ ?	〈電話口で〉~さんいますか？
6	16	*	be in	いる
7	1		in a slump	不調で
7	1	*	down	落ち込んでいる
7	1	*	get over ~	~を克服する
7	2		which way is up	困難な状況から抜け出す方法
7	2	*	go wrong	（物事が）うまくいかない
7	3		be out of one's hands	~の手に負えない
7	3	*	get fired	解雇される
7	3	*	I wish I could －．	－できたらいいのに

INDEX

Song#	対話番号	＊	表現	意味
7	4		go according to plan	計画通りにいく
7	5		get in one's way	〜の邪魔をする
7	6		ruin one's day	〜の一日を台無しにする
7	6	＊	get even with 〜	〜に仕返しする
7	7		make it through 〜	〜を何とか切り抜ける
7	8		big picture	全体像、大局
7	8	＊	focus on 〜	〜に重点的に取り組む
7	9		It's no big deal.	大したことないよ
7	10		lose track of 〜	〜を見失う、〜の現状がわからなくなる
7	11		see eye to eye	意見が一致する
7	12		end up ー ing	結局ーすることになる
7	12		get 〜 across	〜を伝える、〜を理解させる
7	12		tune 〜 out	〜に興味を示さない、〜を無視する
7	12	＊	as usual	いつもの通り
7	12	＊	so 〜 that S V	とても〜なのでSはVする
7	13		break one's heart	〜を悲嘆にくれさせる
7	13	＊	something or other	何か
7	14		down and out	打ちのめされて、どん底で
7	14		It's not the end of the world.	この世の終わりなんかじゃない
7	14		ups and downs	浮き沈み
8	1		now that S V	今やSはVするので
8	1	＊	How about ー ing?	ーするのはどうですか？
8	2		be back on track	元に戻っている
8	2		make up	仲直りする
8	2	＊	call off 〜	〜を取りやめる
8	3		catch one's breath	一息つく
8	4		It's been (such) a long time.	（すごく）久しぶりだ
8	4	＊	What have you been up to?	最近、何してたの？
8	5		unwind	緊張をほぐす
8	5		settle down	落ち着く
8	5	＊	Tell me about it.	その通りだ
8	5	＊	can't wait for 〜 to ー	〜がーするのが待ち遠しい
8	5	＊	be wound up	苛立っている
8	6		even if S V	たとえSがVしても

Song#	対話番号	*	表現	意味
8	6	*	get wet	濡れる
8	7		come up	（問題などが）発生する
8	7	*	What's going on?	どうしたの？
8	7	*	make it to ~	~に出席する
8	8		be in the clear	危機を脱している
8	8	*	get ~ worked out	~がうまくいく
8	8	*	as long as S V	S が V する限りは
8	8	*	mess up	失敗する
8	9		room to breathe	一息つく機会
8	9	*	Are you up for ~ ?	~に乗り気ですか？
8	10		get one's feet back on the ground	元の安定した状態に戻る
8	11		believe in ~	~（の力）を信頼する
8	11		without a doubt	疑いなく
8	11	*	run for ~	~に立候補する
8	12		history	過去のもの
8	12	*	go down the tubes	駄目になる
8	12	*	I bet S V .	きっと S は V する
8	13		as a rule of thumb	経験からいって、指針として
8	14		deal with ~	~に対処する、~を扱う
8	15		catch ~ off guard	~の不意を衝く
8	15	*	get promoted	昇進する
8	16		make a stand	抵抗する
8	17		for a reason	理由があって
8	18		It all comes down to ~ .	（問題は全て）結局~ということになる、~が一番大事ということになる
8	19		The wires get crossed.	誤解が生じる
8	19	*	be supposed to －	ーすることになっている
8	19	*	show up	現れる
8	20		One's point gets lost.	~の言いたいことがわからない
8	21		pack a punch	威力がある、強い影響を及ぼす
8	21		take ~ too far	~をやり過ぎる
8	22		crystal-clear	非常に明瞭な
8	23		fall through	失敗に終わる
8	23		What can you do?	どうしようもない

INDEX

Song#	対話番号	＊	表現	意味
8	23		let it slide	成り行きにまかせる
8	24		give it another try	もう一度やってみる
8	24		give up	諦める

【著者プロフィール】

ジェフリー・ウデン（Geoffrey Wooden）

ハワイ州ホノルル生まれ。
地元のプナホウ高校（Punahou High School）を卒業後、オレゴン大学にて作曲法を専攻。その後、ブリティッシュコロンビア大学にて作曲法の修士号を取得する。
現在は、妻と東京在住。6年間に渡って、日本人の英語指導にあたる傍ら、英語教本の監修やラジオDJもこなす。趣味は、ギター演奏、作曲、読書、料理、ボディーサーフィン、カラオケ、仲間と居酒屋に行くこと。

登内 和夫（とのうち・かずお）

1959年、埼玉県川口市生まれ。
慶應義塾大学卒。42歳で初挑戦したTOEICテストで満点の990点を獲得。豊富な英語指導経験を活かして、高校生用英語テキスト作成や翻訳など、精力的に執筆を手がけている。
著書に『超右脳つぶやき英語トレーニング』（共著）『超右脳おしゃべり英語リスニング』（共著）『超右脳語りかけ英語トレーニング』（共著）『超右脳TOEICテスト入門』（共著）『超右脳つぶやき英語トレーニング留学編』（共著）『A Wonderful Thing』（監修）『英語の本質を楽しく身につけるトレーニングブック』（共著）『超右脳高速「英単語」記憶トレーニング』（共著）（いずれも小社刊）など多数。

装丁：清原一隆（KIYO　DESIGN）
イラスト：テンキ
本文デザイン：松利江子
組版：横内俊彦

> 視覚障害その他の理由で活字のままでこの本を利用出来ない人のために、営利を目的とする場合を除き「録音図書」「点字図書」「拡大図書」等の製作をすることを認めます。その際は著作権者、または、出版社までご連絡ください。

ジェフさんの歌で学ぶ
今日から使える英語表現400

2008年11月5日　初版発行

著　者	ジェフリー・ウデン　登内和夫
発行者	仁部　亨
発行所	総合法令出版株式会社
	〒107-0052　東京都港区赤坂1-9-15
	日本自転車会館2号館7階
	電話　03-3584-9821（代）
	振替　00140-0-69059
印刷・製本	中央精版印刷株式会社

ISBN 978-4-86280-106-7
©Geoffrey Wooden&Kazuo Tonouchi　2008　Printed in Japan
落丁・乱丁本はお取替えいたします。

総合法令出版ホームページ　http://www.horei.com/

好評発売中!!

教育学博士 七田 眞 推薦!!

これほど
音読に適した教材は
ないと言っても
過言ではありません

A Wonderful Thing

Written by　Vincent Marx
Illustated by　Irene Wood
ranslated by　Eriko Marx
Advisor　Kazuo Tonouchi

物語音読CD付き［3倍速も収録］

英語習得のための仕掛けをストーリの中に
意図的にちりばめた、理想的な英語テキスト！

フルカラーの美しいイラストをみて
イメージをふくらませ、
楽しい音声を聴きながらストーリーを
追っていくだけで、英語が上手くなる！！

四六版上製　　88頁　　定価1680円（税込）

英語の本質を楽しく身につける
トレーニングブック
A Womderful Thing　GUIDEBOOK

Written by Vincent Marx ／ 登内和夫

設問実習CD付き

アメリカ言語学者による、
ノンネイティブのための
最も優れた英語教材がここに誕生！

英語を身につけるために最も重要な
英語独特の『リズム』『韻』そして『文化』が
楽しく身につけられる！！

四六版並製　　224頁　　定価1680円（税込）

好評発売中!!

1分間に
数十個もの
英単語が
どんどん頭に入ってくる!

超右脳
高速「英単語」記憶トレーニング

七田 眞／登内 和夫 著
2倍速／4倍速 CD1枚付
A5判並製 320頁 定価1995円(税込み)

　語学学習のポイントは、できるだけ多くの単語をできるだけ速く覚えるところにあります。
　そこで本書の「高速英単語記憶法」を使えば、他の英語教材では類を見ないほど速いスピードで英単語がマスターできるのです。2倍速＆4倍速の高速英単語音声が、あなたの右脳を活性化し、記憶力が劇的に向上します。